COUNTRY MUSIC HALL OF FAME® AND MUSEUM PRESENTS

COUNTRY MUSIC TRIVIA

An Interactive Blvd.™ Book and CD

Compiled by Brian Mansfield

Rutledge Hill Press™
Nashville, Tennessee

A Division of Thomas Nelson, Inc.
www.ThomasNelson.com

Published by Rutledge Hill Press, a Division of Thomas Nelson, Inc., P.O. Box 141000, Nashville, Tennessee 37214.

Design by Creative Access, Inc., Nashville, Tennessee
CD Design by Vision 3, Nashville, Tennessee
Lonestar Photograph courtesy of Russ Harrington
All other photos courtesy of Country Music Hall of Fame®

Library of Congress Cataloging-in-Publication Data
Mansfield, Brian. 1963–
    Country Music Hall of Fame and Museum presents country music trivia : an Interactive Blvd. book and cd / compiled by Brian Mansfield.
        p. cm.
ISBN 1-4016-0121-9 (pbk.)
1. Country music—Miscellanea. 2. Country Music Hall of Fame & Museum (Nashville, Tenn.) I. Title: Country music trivia. II. Country Music Hall of Fame & Museum (Nashville, Tenn.) III. Title.
    ML3524.M362 2003
    782.421642'092'2—dc21

                                                    2003010205

Printed in the United States of America

03 04 05 06 07 — 5 4 3 2 1

TABLE OF CONTENTS

INTRODUCTION BY
LONESTAR

GROWING UP IN TEXAS, we listened to all types of music, but it was country music that stirred our souls.

When we first picked up instruments and began playing, we wanted to tell stories like Waylon Jennings, have fun like Alabama, and warm hearts like Ronnie Milsap.

Country music tells the stories of real people, and real life. Whether it's a love ballad or a honky tonk anthem, it's music we all relate to because at some point we've lived a part of it. Country music is about being true and about how people *really* live their lives. It's songs about those moments that might seem small at the time, but that later turn out to be defining ones in your life. And if you're a musician, and you're lucky, that moment may end up a question in a book like this.

Country Music Trivia is a tribute to those who created country music and to those who still keep you singing along.

As you answer the questions and play the CD game, you'll remember not only the artist or song, but also the first time you heard Patsy Cline, or that summer vacation driving across the country singing to the radio with your dad, or maybe even the time you had your heart broken by your first love. Country music is how we connect; it opens up doors and helps us celebrate our lives.

The Country Music Hall of Fame and Museum celebrates country music and brings it to life, and *Country Music Trivia* makes it fun and entertaining. So enjoy quizzing yourself and your friends . . . and you better get the Lonestar questions right.

TRIVIA
QUIZ

1. **What is Martina McBride's maiden name?**
   A) Grooms   B) Hughes   C) Mariea   D) Schiff

Martina McBride

2. **Who played piano on such records as Hank Locklin's "Please Help Me, I'm Falling," the Browns' "The Three Bells," Don Gibson's "Oh Lonesome Me," and Elvis Presley's "Are You Lonesome Tonight"?**
   A) Owen Bradley   C) Jerry Lee Lewis
   B) Floyd Cramer   D) Hargus "Pig" Robbins

3. **Which member of Diamond Rio previously played bluegrass as a member of J.D. Crowe and the New South?**
   A) Gene Johnson   C) Brian Prout
   B) Jimmy Olander   D) Marty Roe

4. **What was the first country album to yield five #1 singles?**
   A) *No Fences*, Garth Brooks   C) *The Woman in Me*, Shania Twain
   B) *Diamonds and Dirt*, Rodney Crowell   D) *Feels So Right*, Alabama

5. **What famed country announcer lost the Democratic primary for a Tennessee congressional seat to future vice president Al Gore in 1976?**
   A) T. Tommy Cutrer   B) Ralph Emery   C) Hairl Hensley   D) Grant Turner

6. **Who performed country's first million-selling record, "The Wreck of the Old '97" / "The Prisoner's Song"?**
   A) Carter Family   B) Vernon Dalhart   C) Carson Robison   D) Jimmie Rodgers

7. **Inspired by Herb Alpert & the Tijuana Brass, what big band did trumpeter Danny Davis form in 1968?**
   A) Nashville Brass   C) Nashville-Grass
   B) Nashville Cats   D) Nashville Sound

8. **What singer appeared opposite Nick Nolte and Charles Durning as a pro-football quarterback in the 1979 film *North Dallas Forty*?**
   A) Cal Smith   B) Kris Kristofferson   C) Narvel Felts   D) Mac Davis

Answers begin on page 62.

9. **To which Grand Ole Opry star was media personality Ralph Emery married from 1960 to 1964?**
   A) Connie Smith   B) Skeeter Davis   C) Jean Shepard   D) Jeannie Seely

10. **Who played pedal steel on such Ray Price classics as "Crazy Arms," "City Lights," "Invitation to the Blues," and "Heartaches by the Number"?**
    A) Jerry Byrd   B) Jimmy Day   C) Shot Jackson   D) Speedy West

11. **Which singer, one-half of a Hall of Fame brother duo, wrote an autobiography titled *Truth Is Stranger Than Publicity*?**
    A) Bill Carlisle   B) Alton Delmore   C) Phil Everly   D) Charlie Louvin

12. **Which duo's career ended when one of its members was killed in a single-car wreck en route to a memorial service for Patsy Cline, Cowboy Copas, Hawkshaw Hawkins, and Randy Hughes?**
    A) Davis Sisters   B) Delmore Brothers   C) Johnnie & Jack   D) Stanley Brothers

13. **Which singer recorded such pop hits as "Bluer than Blue" and "This Night Won't Last Forever" before topping the country charts with songs like "Give Me Wings" and "The Moon Is Still over Her Shoulder"?**
    A) Paul Davis   B) David Lynn Jones   C) Michael Johnson   D) David Loggins

14. **What did Charlie Rich do with the envelope that proclaimed John Denver the Country Music Association's 1975 Entertainer of the Year?**
    A) He angrily ripped it to shreds.
    B) He wadded it up and threw it into the audience.
    C) He set it afire.
    D) He gave it to Denver as a keepsake.

15. **What group topped the country charts in 1999 with "Amazed"?**
    A) Alabama   B) Diamond Rio   C) Little Texas   D) Lonestar

16. **Who had a #1 hit in 2001 with "Ain't Nothing 'bout You"?**
    A) Garth Brooks   C) Montgomery Gentry
    B) Brooks & Dunn   D) Aaron Tippin

17. **Who spent five weeks at #1 in 1993 with a song titled simply "I Love You"?**
    A) Faith Hill   B) Martina McBride   C) Reba McEntire   D) Jo Dee Messina

Answers begin page 62.

18. **What singer's hits include "Love without End, Amen," "One Night at a Time," and "I've Come to Expect It from You"?**
    A) Alan Jackson   B) Tim McGraw   C) George Strait   D) Randy Travis

19. **Who took "Love Gets Me Every Time" to the #1 spot in 1997?**
    A) Reba McEntire   B) Pam Tillis   C) Shania Twain   D) Trisha Yearwood

20. **What was the Dixie Chicks' first album?**
    A) *Dixie Chicks*   C) *Thank Heavens for Dale Evans*
    B) *Wide Open Spaces*   D) *Fly*

21. **Which former Beatle had a hit duet with Buck Owens?**
    A) George Harrison   B) John Lennon   C) Paul McCartney   D) Ringo Starr

22. **Who replaced William Lee Golden in the Oak Ridge Boys?**
    A) Duane Allen   B) Jimmy Fortune   C) Steve Sanders   D) Richard Sterban

23. **What does the "C." in Jimmy C. Newman stand for?**
    A) Charles   B) Cameron   C) Carl   D) Cajun

24. **Which country singer was married briefly to actress Julia Roberts?**
    A) Steve Earle   B) Lyle Lovett   C) Randy Travis   D) Dwight Yoakam

25. **What was the name of Pam Tillis's debut album?**
    A) *Pam Tillis*   C) *Beyond the Doll of Cutey*
    B) *Put Yourself in My Place*   D) *Tillis*

26. **Who was the first country singer to be a musical guest on *Saturday Night Live*?**
    A) Johnny Cash   B) Kris Kristofferson   C) Anne Murray   D) Willie Nelson

27. **Who immediately preceded Natalie Maines as the Dixie Chicks' lead singer?**
    A) Emily Erwin   B) Sara Hickman   C) Laura Lynch   D) Robin Lynn Macy

28. **In order to get a job playing piano for pop singer Bobby Vee, a young Bob Dylan claimed to have backed another 1950s pop idol who would go on to be a major country star. Who was that other artist?**
    A) Ricky Nelson   B) Jerry Lee Lewis   C) Elvis Presley   D) Conway Twitty

Answers begin on page 62.

29. **What singer was married to Hawkshaw Hawkins when Hawkins died in the 1963 plane crash that also killed Cowboy Copas and Patsy Cline?**
    A) Jean Shepard   B) Jeanne Pruett   C) Jeannie Seely   D) Jan Howard

30. **Who won a Best Actress Oscar for her portrayal of Loretta Lynn in the 1980 film *Coal Miner's Daughter*?**
    A) Beverly D'Angelo   B) Jessica Lange   C) Sissy Spacek   D) Loretta Lynn

31. **Who was the first artist to win the Country Music Association's Entertainer of the Year award?**
    A) Bill Anderson   C) Buck Owens
    B) Eddy Arnold   D) Johnny Cash

32. **What was the name of the band that backed Bill Monroe?**
    A) Blue Grass Boys
    B) Blue Sky Boys
    C) Foggy Mountain Boys
    D) Clinch Mountain Boys

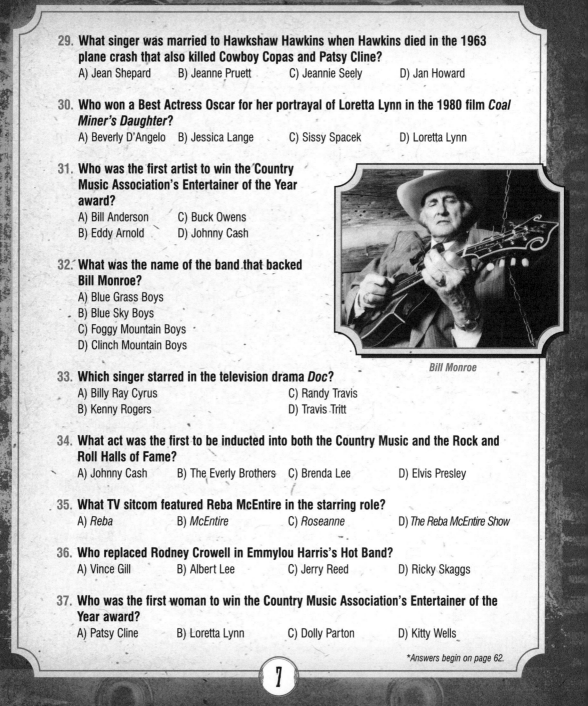

Bill Monroe

33. **Which singer starred in the television drama *Doc*?**
    A) Billy Ray Cyrus   C) Randy Travis
    B) Kenny Rogers   D) Travis Tritt

34. **What act was the first to be inducted into both the Country Music and the Rock and Roll Halls of Fame?**
    A) Johnny Cash   B) The Everly Brothers   C) Brenda Lee   D) Elvis Presley

35. **What TV sitcom featured Reba McEntire in the starring role?**
    A) *Reba*   B) *McEntire*   C) *Roseanne*   D) *The Reba McEntire Show*

36. **Who replaced Rodney Crowell in Emmylou Harris's Hot Band?**
    A) Vince Gill   B) Albert Lee   C) Jerry Reed   D) Ricky Skaggs

37. **Who was the first woman to win the Country Music Association's Entertainer of the Year award?**
    A) Patsy Cline   B) Loretta Lynn   C) Dolly Parton   D) Kitty Wells

*Answers begin on page 62.

38. What was Uncle Dave Macon's primary instrument?
A) Banjo   B) Dulcimer   C) Fiddle   D) Guitar

39. Who jumped off the Tallahatchee Bridge in Bobbie Gentry's 1967 hit "Ode to Billie Joe"?
A) Billie Joe Armstrong   C) Billy Joe Shaver
B) Billie Joe McAllister   D) Billie Joe Spears

40. Which country star's name did Canadian rockers Barenaked Ladies drop on the group's 1998 hit "One Week"?
A) Faith Hill   B) Reba McEntire   C) Dolly Parton   D) LeAnn Rimes

41. Which of these artists was inducted into the Country Music Hall of Fame first?
A) Loretta Lynn   B) Patsy Montana   C) Dolly Parton   D) Tammy Wynette

42. Where was Hank Williams scheduled to play January 1, 1953?
A) Canton, Ohio   C) Knoxville, Tennessee
B) Charleston, West Virginia   D) Oak Hill, West Virginia

43. Which country group was once known originally as Wildcountry?
A) Alabama   B) Diamond Rio   C) Restless Heart   D) Shenandoah

44. Who won the first country Grammy?
A) Johnny Cash   B) Everly Brothers   C) Kingston Trio   D) Marty Robbins

45. Who was the first person inducted into the Country Music Hall of Fame during his lifetime?
A) Roy Acuff   B) Johnny Cash   C) Tex Ritter   D) Ernest Tubb

46. Which artist has placed the most Top Forty singles on the *Billboard* country charts?
A) Eddy Arnold   B) Johnny Cash   C) Merle Haggard   D) George Jones

47. What instrument did Sally Ann Forrester play while briefly a member of Bill Monroe's Blue Grass Boys during the early 1940s?
A) Fiddle   B) Banjo   C) Dobro   D) Accordion

48. Who nicknamed Roy Acuff the "King of Country Music"?
A) Babe Ruth   B) Dizzy Dean   C) George D. Hay   D) Fred Rose

Answers begin on page 62.

49. What record label, home to such artists as Doug Kershaw, Wilma Lee & Stoney Cooper, Ernie Ashworth, Don Gibson, and Roy Acuff, was a subsidiary of Acuff-Rose Publications?

A) Acuff Records   B) Rose Records   C) Hickory Records   D) 16th Avenue Records

50. Who won the Academy of Country Music's first Entertainer of the Year award?

A) Roy Clark   B) Merle Haggard   C) Buck Owens   D) Eddy Arnold

51. Who has been a member of both the Amazing Rhythm Aces and Sawyer Brown?

A) Duncan Cameron   C) Mark Miller
B) Gregg "Hobie" Hubbard   D) Russell Smith

52. Ray Price spent 13 weeks of 1958 and 1959 atop *Billboard's* country singles chart with "City Lights." But a former DJ and sportswriter from Georgia wrote the song and recorded it first for the tiny TNT label. Who was he?

A) Bill Anderson   B) Don Gibson   C) Roger Miller   D) Cal Smith

53. What folk and bluegrass group appeared as the Darling Family on *The Andy Griffith Show*?

A) Blue Grass Boys   C) Hillmen
B) Dillards   D) Greenbriar Boys

54. On what automaker's assembly line did the main character of Johnny Cash's "One Piece at a Time" work?

A) Chevrolet   B) Chrysler   C) Cadillac   D) Ford

55. To which member of the Mavericks was Trisha Yearwood married from 1994 to 1999?

A) Paul Deakin   B) Nick Kane   C) Raul Malo   D) Robert Reynolds

56. What act finally broke Brooks & Dunn's eight-year lock on the Country Music Association's Vocal Duo of the Year award in 2000?

A) Bellamy Brothers   C) Kinleys
B) The Judds   D) Montgomery Gentry

57. What was the first album released by Arista Records' Nashville division?

A) Rob Crosby's *Solid Ground*   C) Alan Jackson's *Here in the Real World*
B) Exile's *Still Standing*   D) Pam Tillis's *Put Yourself in My Place*

*Answers begin on page 62.

58. Who is the only artist to be named Entertainer of the Year by the Country Music Association after being inducted into the Country Music Hall of Fame?

A) Roy Acuff B) Eddy Arnold C) Johnny Cash D) Ernest Tubb

59. Who performed on the pilot episode of *Austin City Limits*?

A) Guy Clark B) Kris Kristofferson C) Willie Nelson D) Jerry Jeff Walker

60. When was the first Fan Fair held?

A) 1970 B) 1971 C) 1972 D) 1973

61. What California town earned the nickname "Nashville West" during the 1960s?

A) Anaheim B) Bakersfield C) Los Angeles D) Tulare

62. What was the first act to play country music on Nashville radio?

A) DeFord Bailey C) Possum Hunters
B) Crook Brothers D) Uncle Jimmy Thompson

63. Who is the only member of Alabama not from Fort Payne, Alabama?

A) Jeff Cook C) Mark Herndon
B) Teddy Gentry D) Randy Owen

64. What fictitious pop singer did Garth Brooks create for a 1999 album?

A) Conrad Birdie C) Chris Gaines
B) Manus Evans D) Stag Preston

65. What *Playboy* cover girl hit #5 in 1975 with the single "Brass Buckles"?

A) Barbi Benton C) Jackie Ray
B) Claudia Jennings D) Crystal Smith

Garth Brooks

66. What famed Nashville club was one of the main settings for the 1993 River Phoenix/Sandra Bullock film *The Thing Called Love*?

A) Station Inn B) Exit/In C) Bluebird Café D) Nashville Palace

67. What was the first group to top *Billboard's* country chart with its debut single?

A) Alabama B) Browns C) Diamond Rio D) Statler Brothers

Answers begin on page 62.

68. What Hall of Fame pitcher recorded a version of "Wabash Cannon Ball" for the North Carolina-based Colonial label?

A) Dizzy Dean   B) Whitey Ford   C) Lefty Grove   D) Satchel Paige

69. What famed gospel quartet initially consisted of Grandpa Jones, Merle Travis, and the Delmore Brothers?

A) Brown's Ferry Four   C) Drifting Pioneers
B) Chuck Wagon Gang   D) Stamps-Baxter Quartet

70. Chris Hillman, a former member of the Byrds and the Flying Burrito Brothers, topped the country charts in the 1980s with what band?

A) Desert Rose Band   C) Shenandoah
B) Highway 101   D) Southern Pacific

71. What Nashville independent record label produced the first recordings of Chet Atkins, Minnie Pearl, Ray Price, and B.B. King?

A) Bullet Records   B) Hickory Records   C) Republic Records   D) Tennessee Records

72. What was the first country album to be certified platinum, for sales of one million copies?

A) Alabama's *Feels So Right*   C) Patsy Cline's *Greatest Hits*
B) Glen Campbell's *Wichita Lineman*   D) *Wanted: The Outlaws*

73. What singer, after preceding Marty Roe in the band that would become Diamond Rio, went on to success as a solo artist?

A) Kenny Chesney   B) Ty Herndon   C) Doug Stone   D) Mark Wills

74. Who nicknamed Little Jimmy Dickens "Tater," after Dickens's single "Take an Old Cold 'Tater (and Wait)"?

A) Hank Penny   B) Hank Snow   C) Hank Thompson   D) Hank Williams

75. Which Hank placed the most records in the Top Forty of *Billboard's* country singles charts?

A) Hank Snow   B) Hank Thompson   C) Hank Williams   D) Hank Williams Jr.

76. Which country singer adopted the stage persona of "The Mysterious Rhinestone Cowboy"?

A) Garth Brooks   B) Glen Campbell   C) David Allan Coe   D) Porter Wagoner

Answers begin on page 62.

77. **Who was the only member of New Grass Revival to stay with the group throughout its lifetime, from 1971 to 1989?**
    A) Curtis Burch   B) Sam Bush   C) Béla Fleck   D) Pat Flynn

78. **Who was Jessi Colter's husband before Waylon Jennings?**
    A) Norman Petty   B) Duane Eddy   C) Tompall Glaser   D) Michael Johnson

79. **What songwriter's credits include such George Strait hits as "Unwound," "The Chair," "Ocean Front Property," and "Nobody in His Right Mind Would've Left Her"?**
    A) Aaron Barker   B) Dean Dillon   C) Jim Lauderdale   D) Curtis Wayne

80. **What famed dobro player is nicknamed "Flux"?**
    A) Mike Auldridge   B) Jerry Douglas   C) Josh Graves   D) Rob Ickes

81. **What country comedian was known for his tag line, "I'm goin' back to the wagon, boys, these shoes are killin' me!"?**
    A) Archie Campbell   C) Whitey Ford (The Duke of Paducah)
    B) Crazy Elmer   D) Rod Brasfield

82. **Which of these Bob Dylan albums was not recorded in Nashville?**
    A) *Blonde on Blonde*   C) *John Wesley Harding*
    B) *Blood on the Tracks*   D) *Nashville Skyline*

83. **What Cajun band backed Mary Chapin Carpenter on her Grammy-winning 1991 hit "Down at the Twist and Shout"?**
    A) Balfa Toujours   C) Wayne Toups & Zydecajun
    B) BeauSoleil   D) Steve Riley & the Mamou Playboys

84. **Which artist has spent the most total weeks at the top of *Billboard's* country singles charts?**
    A) Eddy Arnold   B) Garth Brooks   C) George Jones   D) Hank Williams

85. **What country singer's Arizona gravestone reads, "A vagabond dreamer, a rhymer and a singer of songs, a revolutionary in country music, beloved by the world"?**
    A) Johnny Bond   B) Waylon Jennings   C) Royce Kendall   D) Roger Miller

86. **Under what name did Johnny Paycheck first record?**
    A) Donnie Cash   B) Donald Lytle   C) John Lytle   D) Donnie Young

Answers begin on page 62.

87. When Mark Chesnutt left his regular gig at Cutter's Nightclub in Beaumont, Texas, in 1990, who replaced him?

    A) Tracy Byrd   B) Tracy Lawrence   C) Neal McCoy   D) Clay Walker

88. To whom was June Carter married before Johnny Cash?

    A) Cal Smith   B) Carl Smith   C) Billy Walker   D) Charlie Walker

89. In which Robert Duvall film did June Carter Cash have a part?

    A) *The Apostle*   B) *Days of Thunder*   C) *The Great Santini*   D) *Tender Mercies*

90. Who had Top Ten singles with Emmylou Harris, Keith Whitley, Gus Hardin, and the Pointer Sisters' Anita Pointer as duet partners?

    A) John Conlee
    B) Earl Thomas Conley
    C) Ricky Skaggs
    D) Don Williams

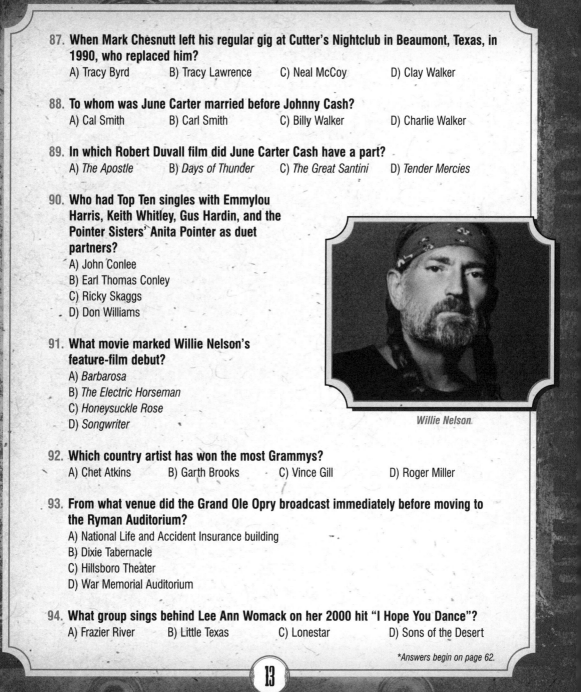

91. What movie marked Willie Nelson's feature-film debut?

    A) *Barbarosa*
    B) *The Electric Horseman*
    C) *Honeysuckle Rose*
    D) *Songwriter*

Willie Nelson.

92. Which country artist has won the most Grammys?

    A) Chet Atkins   B) Garth Brooks   C) Vince Gill   D) Roger Miller

93. From what venue did the Grand Ole Opry broadcast immediately before moving to the Ryman Auditorium?

    A) National Life and Accident Insurance building
    B) Dixie Tabernacle
    C) Hillsboro Theater
    D) War Memorial Auditorium

94. What group sings behind Lee Ann Womack on her 2000 hit "I Hope You Dance"?

    A) Frazier River   B) Little Texas   C) Lonestar   D) Sons of the Desert

Answers begin on page 62.

95. Who recorded "Friends in Low Places," only to have Garth Brooks beat him to the punch by releasing it as a single first?
A) Clint Black   B) Tracy Byrd   C) Kenny Chesney   D) Mark Chesnutt

96. Aside from Charley Pride, which African-American artist has had the most Top Forty country hits?
A) O.B. McClinton   B) Stoney Edwards   C) Big Al Downing   D) Ray Charles

97. Who played steel guitar on Ray Price's "Night Life" and Faron Young's "Sweet Dreams"?
A) Jimmy Day   B) Buddy Emmons   C) Shot Jackson   D) Ralph Mooney

98. What group, after topping the pop charts in 1978 with "Kiss You All Over," went on to have 10 #1 country hits during the 1980s, including "Woke Up in Love"?
A) Exile   B) Highway 101   C) Restless Heart   D) Southern Pacific

99. Who wrote and sang the chart-topping 1972 hits "Funny Face" and "The Happiest Girl in the Whole U.S.A."?
A) Lynn Anderson   B) Barbara Fairchild   C) Donna Fargo   D) Charly McClain

100. What disease, diagnosed in 1979, effectively stalled Donna Fargo's performing career?
A) Amyotrophic lateral sclerosis (ALS)   C) Multiple sclerosis (MS)
B) Breast cancer   D) Muscular dystrophy

101. Whose #1 singles include "Before the Next Teardrop Falls" and "Wasted Days and Wasted Nights"?
A) Glen Campbell   B) Freddy Fender   C) Willie Nelson   D) Johnny Rodriguez

102. What fiddler cut the 1922 sides for Victor that are considered the first country music recordings?
A) Fiddlin' John Carson   C) A.C. "Eck" Robertson
B) Fiddlin' Doc Roberts   D) Uncle Jimmy Thompson

103. Which singer counts "That's the Way" among her hit singles?
A) Jo Dee Messina   B) Lorrie Morgan   C) LeAnn Rimes   D) Lee Ann Womack

104. What act had the first #1 country hit of the 1980s with "Coward of the County"?
A) Larry Gatlin & the Gatlin Brothers   C) Kenny Rogers
B) Oak Ridge Boys   D) T.G. Sheppard

Answers begin on page 62.

105. "My Heart" was a #1 hit in 1980 for which singer?

A) Ronnie Milsap   B) Charley Pride   C) Eddie Rabbitt   D) Don Williams

106. Who won the Country Music Association's Single of the Year award for "Why Not Me"?

A) Janie Fricke   B) The Judds   C) Kendalls   D) Anne Murray

107. What future Country Music Hall of Famer caused controversy with his 1969 single "Okie from Muskogee"?

A) Johnny Cash   B) Merle Haggard   C) Roger Miller   D) Porter Wagoner

108. Whose catch phrase was "Bless your pea-pickin' little heart"?

A) Roy Acuff   B) Minnie Pearl   C) Red Foley   D) Tennessee Ernie Ford

109. What sister group—consisting of Kathy, Kim, Christy, and June—had #1 country hits with songs like "I Fell in Love Again Last Night," "Mama's Never Seen Those Eyes," and "You Again" during the 1980s?

A) Burns Sisters   C) McCarters

B) Forester Sisters   D) Sweethearts of the Rodeo

110. What Country Music Hall of Famer is Lorrie Morgan's father?

A) Harlan Howard   B) Floyd Tillman   C) Hubert Long   D) George Morgan

111. What rock band originally recorded "Hurt," which became a video hit for Johnny Cash in 2003?

A) Danzig   B) Nine Inch Nails   C) Nirvana   D) Soundgarden

112. According to the Lovin' Spoonful's 1966 song "Nashville Cats," how many guitar pickers are there in Nashville?

A) 5,976   C) 1,352

B) 1,534   D) "More than you can shake a stick at"

113. What producer ran Capitol Records' country division from 1951 to 1969, signing such artists as Faron Young, Ferlin Husky, Merle Haggard, and Buck Owens in the process?

A) Jim Denny   B) Bob Ferguson   C) Ken Nelson   D) Jack Stapp

114. In what year did Garth Brooks's first TV special, *This Is Garth Brooks*, air on NBC?

A) 1990   B) 1992   C) 1994   D) 1996

Answers begin on page 62.

115. On January 1, 1959, Johnny Cash played his first free concert for the inmates of San Quentin Prison. What future Country Music Hall of Famer was in the audience at that show?

A) Merle Haggard   B) Merle Travis   C) Cliffie Stone   D) Buck Owens

116. In what movie did Reba McEntire make her feature-film debut?

A) *The Little Rascals*   B) *North*   C) *One Night at McCool's*   D) *Tremors*

117. Which of these country music radio shows went on the air first?

A) *WSM Barn Dance*, Nashville
B) *Renfro Valley Barn Dance*, Cincinnati
C) *WWVA Jamboree*, Wheeling, West Virginia
D) *WLS Barn Dance*, Chicago

Reba McEntire

118. What disease killed Jimmie Rodgers?

A) Cancer   C) Smallpox
B) Pneumonia   D) Tuberculosis

119. What was the first country album to debut at #1 in *Billboard's* Top 200 album chart?

A) Garth Brooks's *No Fences*
B) Garth Brooks's *Ropin' the Wind*
C) Billy Ray Cyrus's *Some Gave All*
D) Shania Twain's *Come on Over*

120. Steve Wariner has a middle name that reflects his birthday—Christmas Day 1954. What is it?

A) Kris   B) Nicholas   C) Noel   D) Yule

121. What western swing bandleader was sentenced to life in prison for the murder of his wife?

A) Bill Boyd   B) Milton Brown   C) Spade Cooley   D) Leon McAuliffe

122. Who played steel guitar on Lefty Frizzell's "Always Late (with Your Kisses)"?

A) Curly Chalker   C) Ralph Mooney
B) Leon McAuliffe   D) Joaquin Murphey

123. Which NASCAR driver is mentioned in Kenny Chesney's hit "How Forever Feels"?

A) Jeff Gordon   B) Richard Petty   C) Tony Stewart   D) Darrell Waltrip

Answers begin on page 62.

124. What British rock group asked Vince Gill to join as one of its guitarists?
A) Dexy's Midnight Runners   C) Pet Shop Boys
B) Dire Straits   D) The Police

125. Which of these siblings of more famous stars had the most Top Forty hits?
A) Tommy Cash   B) Louise Mandrell   C) Pake McEntire   D) Stella Parton

126. Which country singer married noted session bassist and producer Emory Gordy Jr.?
A) Rosanne Cash   B) Emmylou Harris   C) Patty Loveless   D) Kathy Mattea

127. Which member of Shenandoah formerly played guitar for the r&b group Funkadelic?
A) Ralph Ezell   B) Marty Raybon   C) Jim Seales   D) Stan Thorn

128. In the first line of "I Like It, I Love It," how much did Tim McGraw say he spent last night at the county fair?
A) $29   B) $48   C) $58   D) $110

129. Vince Gill's first hit came as the lead singer of what pop group?
A) Air Supply   B) Little River Band   C) Pure Prairie League   D) Toto

130. What NASCAR driver appeared with Brooks & Dunn in their "Honky Tonk Truth" video?
A) Dale Earnhardt   B) Richard Petty   C) Bobby LaBonte   D) Darrell Waltrip

131. What flavor Sno-Cone did Alan Jackson settle for in "Chattahoochee"?
A) Cherry   B) Lemon   C) Grape   D) Blue Raspberry

132. Which country artist also raced on the NASCAR circuit?
A) Billy "Crash" Craddock   C) Marty Robbins
B) Ronnie Dunn   D) Joe Stampley

133. Who had a platinum-selling single with "Elvira"?
A) Rodney Crowell   B) Dallas Frazier   C) Oak Ridge Boys   D) Statler Brothers

134. Who crossed over to the pop charts in 1986 with the song "Bop"?
A) John Anderson   B) Mac Davis   C) Paul Davis   D) Dan Seals

135. Who topped the charts in 1996 with her single "Strawberry Wine"?
A) Deana Carter   B) Jo Dee Messina   C) LeAnn Rimes   D) Mindy McCready

Answers begin on page 62.

136. **Who won Single of the Year awards from both the Academy of Country Music and the Country Music Association for "When I Call Your Name"?**
    A) Clint Black   B) Vince Gill   C) Ricky Van Shelton   D) Keith Whitley

137. **Whose "A Little Good News" won her the Country Music Association's Single of the Year in 1984?**
    A) Janie Fricke   B) Crystal Gayle   C) Anne Murray   D) Dolly Parton

138. **What mythical Tennessee town did Minnie Pearl claim as her home?**
    A) Bucksnort   B) Centerville   C) Grinder's Switch   D) Wartrace

139. **What was the name of Roy Rogers's horse?**
    A) Champion   B) Silver   C) Topper   D) Trigger

140. **Who sings with Shania Twain on the original album version of "From This Moment On"?**
    A) Garth Brooks   B) Toby Keith   C) Sammy Kershaw   D) Bryan White

141. **In what Broadway musical did Reba McEntire star in 2001?**
    A) *42nd Street*   B) *Annie Get Your Gun*   C) *Cats*   D) *Oklahoma*

142. **Seven members of what singer's touring band were killed in a 1991 plane crash?**
    A) Wynonna Judd   B) Reba McEntire   C) Lorrie Morgan   D) Trisha Yearwood

143. **What group won the Academy of Country Music's Single of the Year award in 1979 for "All the Gold in California"?**
    A) Dave & Sugar   B) Larry Gatlin & the Gatlin Brothers
    C) Oak Ridge Boys   D) Statler Brothers

144. **With which pop act did Dan Seals record before finding solo success as a country singer?**
    A) Danny & the Juniors   C) England Dan & John Ford Coley
    B) Danleers   D) Seals & Crofts

145. **What pop singer co-wrote the Lonestar hit "You Walked In"?**
    A) Bryan Adams   B) Ryan Adams   C) Phil Collins   D) Brian McKnight

146. **Which of these artists entered the Top Forty of *Billboard's* country singles chart first?**
    A) Clint Black   B) Garth Brooks   C) Alan Jackson   D) Travis Tritt

Answers begin on page 62.

147. Which act has received the most nominations for the Country Music Association's Entertainer of the Year—without ever winning the award?

A) Randy Travis   B) The Judds   C) Kenny Rogers   D) Waylon Jennings

148. What was the amount on the price tag that hung from Minnie Pearl's straw hat?

A) 69¢   B) $1.98   C) $2.49   D) $5.00

149. What country act's hits include "Wide Open Spaces" and "I Can Love You Better"?

A) Dixie Chicks   C) SHeDAISY

B) Sara Evans   D) Lee Ann Womack

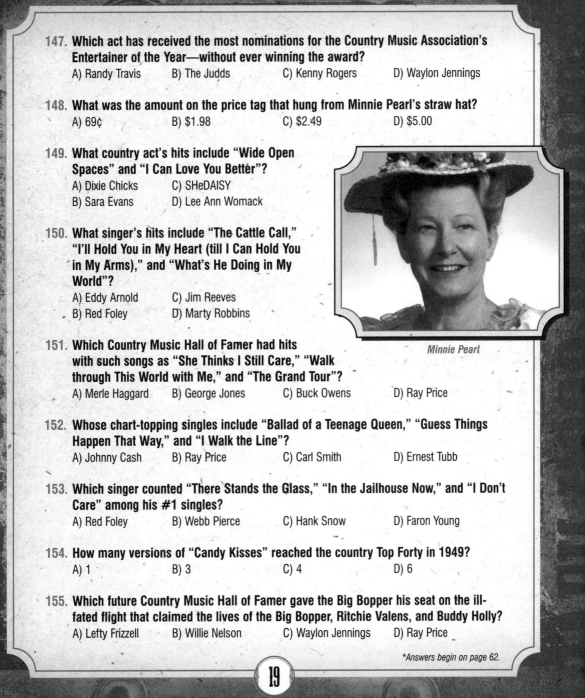

150. What singer's hits include "The Cattle Call," "I'll Hold You in My Heart (till I Can Hold You in My Arms)," and "What's He Doing in My World"?

A) Eddy Arnold   C) Jim Reeves

B) Red Foley   D) Marty Robbins

Minnie Pearl

151. Which Country Music Hall of Famer had hits with such songs as "She Thinks I Still Care," "Walk through This World with Me," and "The Grand Tour"?

A) Merle Haggard   B) George Jones   C) Buck Owens   D) Ray Price

152. Whose chart-topping singles include "Ballad of a Teenage Queen," "Guess Things Happen That Way," and "I Walk the Line"?

A) Johnny Cash   B) Ray Price   C) Carl Smith   D) Ernest Tubb

153. Which singer counted "There Stands the Glass," "In the Jailhouse Now," and "I Don't Care" among his #1 singles?

A) Red Foley   B) Webb Pierce   C) Hank Snow   D) Faron Young

154. How many versions of "Candy Kisses" reached the country Top Forty in 1949?

A) 1   B) 3   C) 4   D) 6

155. Which future Country Music Hall of Famer gave the Big Bopper his seat on the ill-fated flight that claimed the lives of the Big Bopper, Ritchie Valens, and Buddy Holly?

A) Lefty Frizzell   B) Willie Nelson   C) Waylon Jennings   D) Ray Price

Answers begin on page 62.

156. Which major-league baseball team did singing cowboy Gene Autry own?

A) Anaheim Angels
B) Houston Astros
C) Los Angeles Dodgers
D) Texas Rangers

157. Which singer led a double life from 1969 to 1971, both as a member of the rock group Paul Revere & the Raiders and as the performer of such country hits as "These Are Not My People" and "Games People Play"?

A) Jerry Reed
B) Billy Joe Royal
C) Joe South
D) Freddy Weller

158. Which bluegrass duo recorded the theme for the 1960s TV sitcom, *The Beverly Hillbillies*?

A) Flatt & Scruggs
B) Jim & Jesse
C) Stanley Brothers
D) Monroe Brothers

159. How old was Louis Marshall Jones when he created his "Grandpa Jones" character?

A) 22
B) 31
C) 47
D) 54

160. What year were the letters in "He Stopped Loving Her Today" dated?

A) 1962
B) 1964
C) 1972
D) 1980

161. Who turned down an invitation to the Pittsburgh Pirates' spring training camp in order to join the *Louisiana Hayride*?

A) Roy Acuff
B) Bob Luman
C) Charley Pride
D) Jim Reeves

162. What honky-tonk singer was billed as "eleven-and-a-half yards of personality"?

A) Hawkshaw Hawkins
B) Moon Mullican
C) Justin Tubb
D) Johnny Horton

163. What inspired Harley Allen to write the 2000 John Michael Montgomery hit "The Little Girl"?

A) A television program
B) An Internet chain letter
C) A newspaper story
D) A sermon

164. What instrument did Emmylou Harris play in her high school marching band?

A) Flute
B) Piccolo
C) Alto saxophone
D) Bass clarinet

165. What singer is known as "Whisperin' Bill"?

A) Bill Anderson
B) Bill Carlisle
C) Bill Monroe
D) Billy Walker

Answers begin on page 62.

166. What future Country Music Association Entertainer of the Year got his first music-industry job in the mailroom of The Nashville Network (TNN)?
A) Garth Brooks   B) Vince Gill   C) Alan Jackson   D) Tim McGraw

167. What caused Jim Reeves's death?
A) Car crash   C) Alcohol poisoning
B) Plane crash   D) Self-inflicted gunshot wound

168. Who wrote Jeannie C. Riley's million-selling 1968 hit "Harper Valley P.T.A."?
A) Tom T. Hall   B) Kris Kristofferson   C) Billy Joe Shaver   D) James Talley

169. What singer had a nine-week chart-topper in 1966 with "Almost Persuaded"?
A) Eddy Arnold   B) Jack Greene   C) David Houston   D) Sonny James

170. Who is known as the "dean of country songwriters"?
A) Hank Cochran   B) Harlan Howard   C) Bob McDill   D) Sonny Throckmorton

171. How much did RCA pay Sun Records' Sam Phillips to buy out Elvis Presley's contract in 1955?
A) $35,000   B) $40,000   C) $300,000   D) $1 million

172. Who sang the ghostly, female obbligato line during the recitation in George Jones's "He Stopped Loving Her Today"?
A) Anita Kerr   B) Millie Kirkham   C) Charly McClain   D) Tammy Wynette

173. Complete this Dolly Parton quote: "There's really only three real female singers in the world: Streisand, Ronstadt, and _____. The rest of us are only pretending."
A) Patsy Cline   B) Jeannie Seely   C) Connie Smith   D) Tammy Wynette

174. How were the members of country duo Johnnie & Jack, whose hits included "Poison Love" and "(Oh Baby Mine) I Get So Lonely," related?
A) Brothers   C) Cousins
B) Brothers-in-law   D) They weren't related

175. Which member of Highway 101 was the child of a Country Music Hall of Famer?
A) Paulette Carlson   C) Curtis Stone
B) Scott "Cactus" Moser   D) Jack Daniels

Answers begin on page 62.

176. Of what television news anchor did Toby Keith say, "I find it interesting that he's not from the U.S."?
A) Tom Brokaw   B) Peter Jennings   C) Dan Rather   D) Wolf Blitzer

177. Waylon Jennings's *Honky Tonk Heroes* album consists mostly of tunes by which Texas singer-songwriter?
A) Ray Wylie Hubbard
B) Willis Alan Ramsey
C) Billy Joe Shaver
D) Jerry Jeff Walker

Waylon Jennings

178. Of whom did Ralph Emery once say, "She has the brains of a computer, the heart of an artist, and the spirit of a minister"?
A) Loretta Lynn
B) Reba McEntire
C) Dolly Parton
D) Tammy Wynette

179. Where is Luckenbach, Texas, located?
A) North of Dallas
B) South of Houston
C) East of San Antonio
D) West of Austin

180. What member of the Country Music Hall of Fame sang such hits as "I Don't Hurt Anymore," "The Rhumba Boogie," and "Hello Love"?
A) Lefty Frizzell
B) Webb Pierce
C) Hank Snow
D) Hank Thompson

181. What singer had huge hits both with honky-tonk numbers like "Crazy Arms" and lush ballads like "For the Good Times"?
A) Roger Miller   B) Willie Nelson   C) Ray Price   D) Cal Smith

182. What singer's hits include "My Heroes Have Always Been Cowboys" and "On the Road Again"?
A) Johnny Cash   B) Waylon Jennings   C) Kris Kristofferson   D) Willie Nelson

183. For a while during the 1970s, Owen Bradley ran Decca/MCA's Nashville operations, and his son, Jerry Bradley, headed the Nashville division of another record company. What was that other label?
A) Capitol   B) CBS   C) Elektra   D) RCA

Answers begin on page 62.

184. What singer had more than a dozen #1 hits between 1974 and 1986, including "'Til the Rivers All Run Dry" and "I Believe in You"?

A) Tom T. Hall   B) Sonny James   C) Conway Twitty   D) Don Williams

185. What singer was seriously injured in a 1975 fall from a Montana mountain?

A) Ed Bruce   B) David Houston   C) Eddy Raven   D) Hank Williams Jr.

186. What singer both wrote and sang the country classics "Cold, Cold Heart" and "Your Cheatin' Heart"?

A) Lefty Frizzell   B) Leon Payne   C) Hank Snow   D) Hank Williams

187. During the 1940s, what entertainer spent more than 40 weeks atop at least one *Billboard* chart with hits like "Pistol Packin' Mama," "Guitar Polka," and "I'm Losing My Mind Over You"?

A) Al Dexter   B) Louis Jordan   C) Ernest Tubb   D) Bob Wills

188. Who produced such Garth Brooks albums as *No Fences*, *Ropin' the Wind*, and *The Chase*?

A) Jimmy Bowen   C) Garth Fundis
B) "Cowboy" Jack Clement   D) Allen Reynolds

189. Who plays the nylon-string guitar part on Marty Robbins's "El Paso"?

A) Harold Bradley   B) Ray Edenton   C) Hank Garland   D) Grady Martin

190. "Summertime Blues," a #1 hit for Alan Jackson in 1994, had previously been a Top Ten pop hit for what 1950s rock & roller?

A) Eddie Cochran   B) Bill Haley   C) Jack Scott   D) Gene Vincent

191. Who said, "Country music is three chords and the truth"?

A) Connie B. Gay   B) Harlan Howard   C) George Jones   D) Hank Williams

192. What singer roomed with Hank Williams and used Williams's Drifting Cowboys as his backup band?

A) Johnny Horton   B) Autry Inman   C) George Morgan   D) Ray Price

193. What country singer was also a world champion bareback bronco rider?

A) Garth Brooks   C) George Strait
B) Chris LeDoux   D) John Michael Montgomery

*Answers begin on page 62.

194. To what country singer was Priscilla Mitchell, Roy Drusky's duet partner in the 1965 chart-topping cheating song "Yes, Mr. Peters," married?

A) Roy Drusky   B) Price Mitchell   C) Jerry Reed   D) Mitchell Torok

195. What country singer played lead parts in New York productions of the musicals *La Bohème* and *Les Misérables*?

A) Earl Thomas Conley   C) Gary Morris
B) Lee Greenwood   D) John Schneider

196. Who spent 10 weeks at #1 in 1960 with "Wings of a Dove"?

A) Roy Acuff   B) Ferlin Husky   C) Hank Locklin   D) Marty Robbins

197. What singing cowboy also narrated more than 50 Disney films and television shows?

A) Rex Allen   B) Smiley Burnette   C) Herb Jeffries   D) Jimmy Wakely

198. Who played steel guitar on Webb Pierce's 1954 hit "Slowly"?

A) Bud Isaacs   B) Buddy Emmons   C) Herb Remington   D) Don Helms

199. Mike Reid, the singer-songwriter whose credits include Ronnie Milsap's "Stranger in My House" and his own "Walk on Faith," was an all-pro lineman for what football team?

A) Cincinnati Bengals   B) Cleveland Browns   C) Houston Oilers   D) Pittsburgh Steelers

200. Why was the date October 2, 1954, significant in Elvis Presley's career?

A) It was the date of his first television appearance.
B) It was the date his first record was released.
C) It was the date he made his first record.
D) It was the date he made his only Grand Ole Opry appearance.

201. What singer had a country hit with "The Wind Beneath My Wings" in 1983, six years before Bette Midler made the song an international pop smash?

A) Nanci Griffith   B) Barbara Mandrell   C) Gary Morris   D) Kenny Rogers

202. Who has a pretty young daughter in Claude King's 1962 hit "Wolverton Mountain"?

A) Clifton Clowers   B) Cliff Clavin   C) Jerry Clower   D) Cliffie Stone

203. To what singer's "worn-out tape" is Garth Brooks listening in "Much Too Young (to Feel This Damn Old)"?

A) Dan Fogelberg   B) Chris LeDoux   C) George Strait   D) James Taylor

Answers begin on page 62.

204. What was the name of the fiddle player who won the golden fiddle in Charlie Daniels's "The Devil Went Down to Georgia"?
A) Bobby B) Charlie C) Johnny D) Ronnie

205. Who is known as "the" Man in Black?
A) Bill Black B) Clint Black C) Johnny Cash D) Merle Haggard

206. What singer was known as "the" Round Mound of Sound?
A) Joe Diffie C) Johnny Russell
B) Kenny Price D) Lulu Roman

207. What singer had his first #1 hit with "Sticks and Stones"?
A) Trace Adkins C) Tracy Lawrence
B) Tracy Byrd D) Toby Keith

208. What did Priscilla Presley give Elvis Presley for their first anniversary?
A) His famed "Solid Gold" Cadillac
B) A grand piano covered in 24-karat gold leaf
C) A baby daughter, Lisa Marie
D) A solid-gold necklace with a lightning bolt and "TCB" on it

Elvis Presley

209. Which singer worked as a tour guide at the Country Music Hall of Fame and Museum?
A) Deana Carter B) Nanci Griffith C) Kathy Mattea D) K.T. Oslin

210. Which of these singers had six singles top the country charts after his or her death?
A) Patsy Cline B) Jim Reeves C) Keith Whitley D) Hank Williams

211. What kind of stain did Tim McGraw have on his white T-shirt in his hit "Something Like That"?
A) Barbecue B) Blood C) Ketchup D) Wine

212. What Shreveport, Louisiana, radio station broadcast the *Louisiana Hayride*?
A) KDAQ B) KWKH C) KLSA D) KITT

Answers begin on page 62.

213. Who was Nashville's first full-time session drummer?
A) Eddie Bayers   B) Buddy Harman   C) Larrie Londin   D) Jerry Wiggins

214. Who left Restless Heart to find solo chart success as the singer of such songs as "Alright Already" and "I'll Cry Tomorrow"?
A) Paul Gregg   B) Dave Innis   C) Larry Stewart   D) Verlon Thompson

215. Which Lonestar album yielded four consecutive #1 singles?
A) *Lonestar*   B) *Crazy Nights*   C) *Lonely Grill*   D) *I'm Already There*

216. As he begins his trucking journey in "Six Days on the Road," what city does Dave Dudley pull out of?
A) Pawtucket   B) Philadelphia   C) Pittsburgh   D) Portland

217. What disease did Naomi Judd contract that prompted The Judds' 1991 farewell tour?
A) Breast cancer   B) Hepatitis   C) Lupus   D) Multiple sclerosis

218. From what Canadian province does Anne Murray hail?
A) New Brunswick   B) Nova Scotia   C) Manitoba   D) Ontario

219. In his 1959 chart-topper "El Paso," what Mexican girl did Marty Robbins fall in love with?
A) Dorinda   B) Felina   C) Maria   D) Rosalita

220. Who sang the 1987 hit "80's Ladies"?
A) Holly Dunn   B) K.T. Oslin   C) Marie Osmond   D) Judy Rodman

221. What product sponsored the half-hour segment of the Grand Ole Opry that broadcast over the NBC radio network beginning in 1939?
A) Crazy Water Crystals   C) Martha White Flour
B) Goo Goo Candy Clusters   D) Prince Albert Smoking Tobacco

222. What singer was nicknamed "the Cherokee Cowboy"?
A) Eddie Dean   B) Ray Price   C) Marvin Rainwater   D) Hank Thompson

223. Whose Top Forty country hits included such songs as "Occasional Wife," "Unmitigated Gall," and "Wonderful World of Women"?
A) Bill Anderson   B) Bob Luman   C) Mel Tillis   D) Faron Young

*Answers begin on page 62.

224. Which singer did then-California governor Ronald Reagan pardon for his criminal record, which included second-degree burglary?
    A) Buck Owens   B) Johnny Paycheck   C) Merle Haggard   D) Wynn Stewart

225. Who recorded the original version of "Ring of Fire," albeit under a different song title?
    A) Anita Carter   B) June Carter   C) Merle Kilgore   D) Carl Smith

226. What radio show did Ernest Tubb begin broadcasting from his Nashville record store in 1947?
    A) *The Ernest Tubb Show*   C) *The Midnight Jamboree*
    B) *Live From Ernest Tubb's*   D) *Tubb Full of Tunes*

227. Who was the youngest country artist ever elected to the Country Music Association's board of directors?
    A) Billy Gilman   B) Brenda Lee   C) Mindy McCready   D) Jo Dee Messina

228. What's the last name of bluegrass brother duo Jim & Jesse?
    A) James   B) McReynolds   C) Monroe   D) Reno

229. Which of these tribute albums did Merle Haggard release first?
    A) *Same Train, a Different Time: Merle Haggard Sings the Great Songs of Jimmie Rodgers*
    B) *A Tribute to the Best Damn Fiddle Player in the World (or, My Salute to Bob Wills)*
    C) *My Farewell to Elvis*
    D) *I Love Dixie Blues … So I Recorded Live in New Orleans*

230. How is Sammy Kershaw related to Cajun fiddler Doug Kershaw?
    A) Brother   B) Cousin   C) Nephew   D) Son

231. Who replaced Paulette Carlson in Highway 101?
    A) Lane Brody   B) Donna Meade   C) Nikki Nelson   D) Marsha Thornton

232. What guitarist was best known for his role as sideman and harmony vocalist in Buck Owens's Buckaroos?
    A) Roy Nichols   B) Don Rich   C) Norm Stephens   D) Redd Volkaert

233. Which singer-songwriter was once Dolly Parton's brother-in-law?
    A) Craig Bickhardt   B) Fred Knobloch   C) Paul Overstreet   D) Thom Schuyler

Answers begin on page 62.

234. **What publishing company, formed by an ownership team that included Ray Price, helped launch the songwriting careers of Hank Cochran, Harlan Howard, and Willie Nelson?**
    A) Cedarwood Publishing Company
    B) Combine Music Publishing
    C) Pamper Music
    D) Tree International

235. **What country comedy duo hit it big with song satires like "(How Much Is) That Hound Dog in the Window" and "The Battle of Kookamonga"?**
    A) Homer & Jethro
    B) Pinkard & Bowden
    C) Lonzo & Oscar
    D) Jamup & Honey

236. **Patty Loveless is a distant cousin of what Country Music Hall of Famer?**
    A) Loretta Lynn
    B) Dolly Parton
    C) Porter Wagoner
    D) Tammy Wynette

237. **What was the first theater built on "The Strip" in Branson, Missouri?**
    A) Grand Palace
    B) Moon River Theatre
    C) Presley's Jubilee
    D) Shoji Tabuchi Theatre

Homer & Jethro

238. **Singer-songwriter Stuart Hamblen, who penned such songs as "This Ole House" and "It Is No Secret," unsuccessfully ran for president on what ticket in 1952?**
    A) Democratic Party
    B) Libertarian Party
    C) Prohibition Party
    D) Republican Party

239. **What is currently Nashville's oldest existing recording studio?**
    A) Javelina Recording Studio
    B) Ocean Way
    C) RCA Studio B
    D) Woodland Studios

240. **What entertainer once signed autographs at Fan Fair for 23 consecutive hours?**
    A) Garth Brooks
    B) Kenny Chesney
    C) Reba McEntire
    D) Shania Twain

241. **What country music journalist is said to have coined the term "Outlaw" to describe the music of Waylon Jennings, Willie Nelson, Tompall Glaser, and others during the 1970s?**
    A) Jack Hurst
    B) Charlie Lamb
    C) Robert K. Oermann
    D) Hazel Smith

Answers begin on page 62.

242. **What country singer played piano and sang backing vocals on Elvis Presley's "Kentucky Rain"?**
    A) Mickey Gilley   B) Jerry Lee Lewis   C) Ronnie Milsap   D) Eddie Rabbitt

243. **Who was the first country entertainer to guest-host *The Tonight Show*?**
    A) Eddy Arnold   B) Johnny Cash   C) Roy Clark   D) Vince Gill

244. **Which of these is not one of the Gatlin Brothers?**
    A) Larry Gatlin   B) Steve Gatlin   C) Rudy Gatlin   D) Gary Gatlin

245. **What singer had 16 consecutive #1 records between 1967 and 1972, including remakes of songs that had been pop hits for Petula Clark, Roy Orbison, and Jimmy Reed?**
    A) Glen Campbell   B) Bobby Goldsboro   C) Sonny James   D) Conway Twitty

246. **What vocal group's members have included Gordon Stoker, Neal Matthews, Hoyt Hawkins, and Ray Walker?**
    A) Anita Kerr Singers   C) Sons of the Pioneers
    B) Jordanaires   D) Statler Brothers

247. **What western swing bandleader worked for a while as Roy Rogers's movie stand-in?**
    A) Hank Penny   B) Johnnie Lee Wills   C) Spade Cooley   D) Leon McAuliffe

248. **What was the singer's CB handle in C.W. McCall's chart-topping 1975 hit "Convoy"?**
    A) Crispy Critter   B) Rubber Duck   C) Teddy Bear   D) White Knight

249. **Which entertainer appeared as Lucy Ricardo's country "Cousin Ernie" on *I Love Lucy*?**
    A) Eddy Arnold   C) Tex Ritter
    B) Tennessee Ernie Ford   D) "T" Texas Tyler

250. **What singer published *Music City News* during the 1960s?**
    A) Eddy Arnold   B) Ernie Ashworth   C) Webb Pierce   D) Faron Young

251. **Who were the first women to make a country record?**
    A) Samantha Bumgarner and Eva Davis   C) Coon Creek Girls
    B) Sara and Maybelle Carter   D) Montana Cowgirls

*Answers begin on page 62.

252. **The members of what country act appeared as crowd-scene extras in *More American Graffiti*?**
A) Dave & Sugar   B) Forester Sisters   C) The Judds   D) Statler Brothers

253. **For what Tony Award-winning musical did Roger Miller write the score?**
A) *Amen Corner*
B) *Big River*
C) *The Mystery of Edwin Drood*
D) *Sunday in the Park with George*

254. **What kind of pie does Alabama sing about in "Song of the South"?**
A) Apple   B) Chess   C) Humble   D) Sweet potato

255. **What bluegrass act recorded a tribute to rock & roller Chuck Berry, naming the album *Berry Pickin' in the Country*?**
A) Dillards
B) Jim & Jesse
C) The Osborne Brothers
D) Reno & Smiley

256. **What was Gene Autry's first movie?**
A) *In Old Santa Fe*
B) *Mystery Mountain*
C) *The Phantom Empire*
D) *Tumbling Tumbleweeds*

257. **What was Faron Young's nickname?**
A) The Youngster   B) Faron Away   C) The Young Sheriff   D) Little Banty Rooster

258. **What singer has co-produced albums for Jo Dee Messina?**
A) Clint Black   B) Alan Jackson   C) Tim McGraw   D) Vince Gill

259. **What singer's early jobs included working as an oil-field worker, a rodeo hand, and a defensive end for a semi-pro football team?**
A) Ronnie Dunn   B) Chris Cagle   C) Toby Keith   D) Tim McGraw

260. **Who had a Top Forty country hit inspired by the movie *Star Wars* during 1977 and 1978?**
A) Billy "Crash" Craddock
B) Dave & Sugar
C) Tom T. Hall
D) Joe Stampley

261. **What singer, whose hits include "Yes!" and "Ordinary Life," briefly worked as a professional wrestler?**
A) Chad Brock   B) Kenny Chesney   C) Ty Herndon   D) Tracy Lawrence

Answers begin on page 62.

262. **In the George Jones hit "The Race Is On," what gets "scratched for another's sake"?**
   A) My tears   B) My heart   C) True love   D) Heartaches

263. **To which member of the television drama *Dallas* cast was Johnny Lee briefly married?**
   A) Linda Gray   B) Lesley-Anne Down   C) Victoria Principal   D) Charlene Tilton

264. **What singer sold T-shirts for Garth Brooks during his 1991 tour and opened for Brooks during his 1992 tour?**
   A) Susan Ashton   B) Martina McBride   C) Victoria Shaw   D) Trisha Yearwood

265. **What singer had her first charting record in 1979, but didn't have her first #1 hit until "Five Minutes" topped the charts in 1990?**
   A) Carlene Carter   B) Rosanne Cash   C) Lorrie Morgan   D) Pam Tillis

266. **In what state was Clint Black born?**
   A) California   C) Texas
   B) New Jersey   D) Tennessee

267. **What honky-tonker managed a Top Ten hit in 1957 with a countrified version of the Everly Brothers' "Bye, Bye Love" that entered the country Top Forty just two weeks after the original?**
   A) Johnny Bond   C) Webb Pierce
   B) Leon Payne   D) Ernest Tubb

Clint Black

268. **What singer's first record, cut for Starday Records in 1954, was called "No Money in This Deal"?**
   A) Arlie Duff   B) George Jones   C) Webb Pierce   D) Red Sovine

269. **According to a 1974 hit by Johnny Russell, who got baptized "in Cedar Creek last Sunday"?**
   A) Jessi Colter   B) Dallas Frazier   C) Whitey Shafer   D) Jesse Taylor

270. **Which of these artists was never a member of Ray Price's backup band?**
   A) Jack Greene   B) Roger Miller   C) Willie Nelson   D) Johnny Paycheck

Answers begin on page 62.

271. **What country singer starred opposite Burt Reynolds in *W.W. and the Dixie Dance Kings* and appeared in all three *Smokey and the Bandit* movies?**
    A) Mac Davis   B) Kris Kristofferson   C) Willie Nelson   D) Jerry Reed

272. **Which of these collaborations did Willie Nelson release first?**
    A) Willie Nelson & Leon Russell, *One for the Road*
    B) Willie Nelson & Ray Price, *San Antonio Rose*
    C) Willie Nelson & Roger Miller, *Old Friends*
    D) Willie Nelson & Faron Young, *Funny How Time Slips Away*

273. **What does Aaron Tippin have tattooed on his right bicep?**
    A) A bald eagle
    B) A heart emblazoned with the name of his wife, Thea
    C) A hula dancer
    D) A palmetto tree and a crescent moon

274. **How many movies did Elvis Presley make?**
    A) 12   B) 19   C) 27   D) 33

275. **How old was K.T. Oslin when she had her first Top Forty hit?**
    A) 19   B) 27   C) 45   D) 52

276. **How old is Delta Dawn in the Tanya Tucker hit of the same name?**
    A) 21   B) 31   C) 41   D) 51

277. **How did Barbara Mandrell bill her October 23, 1997, farewell concert?**
    A) "Do Right One Last Time"   C) "Standing Room Only"
    B) "The Last Dance"   D) "Till You're Gone"

278. **When did the Country Music Hall of Fame open?**
    A) April 1, 1966   B) April 1, 1967   C) April 1, 1968   D) April 1, 1969

279. **How did Keith Whitley die?**
    A) Accidental electrocution   C) Car wreck
    B) Alcohol poisoning   D) Drug overdose

280. **What singer opened a record store in downtown Nashville in 1947?**
    A) Roy Acuff   B) Eddy Arnold   C) Webb Pierce   D) Ernest Tubb

Answers begin on page 62.

281. In John Anderson's "Swingin'," who's "as pretty as the angels when they sing"?
A) Shirley Thompson
B) Charlotte Johnson
C) Becky Thompson
D) Becky Talbot

282. What country singer drew on the hog-farming experiences of his youth and launched a successful sausage-making company, now owned by the Sara Lee Corporation?
A) Jimmy Day
B) Billy Dean
C) Eddie Dean
D) Jimmy Dean

283. In what year did *Hee Haw* first air?
A) 1969
B) 1970
C) 1971
D) 1972

284. What Nashville radio station broadcasts the Grand Ole Opry?
A) WKDF
B) WPLN
C) WSIX
D) WSM

285. What famed country bandleader of the 1940s wrote such standards as "Born to Lose," "No Letter Today," and "I've Got Five Dollars and It's Saturday Night"?
A) Ted Daffan
B) Al Dexter
C) Floyd Tillman
D) Jimmy Wakely

286. What singer once worked as a private plane pilot for corporate executives?
A) Mark Chesnutt
B) Alan Jackson
C) Clint Black
D) Aaron Tippin

287. When was the country music cable channel CMT launched?
A) August 1, 1981
B) August 1, 1982
C) March 6, 1983
D) March 6, 1984

288. In which Jack Nicholson film do Tammy Wynette's "Stand by Your Man" and "D-I-V-O-R-C-E" figure prominently?
A) *Ironweed*
B) *As Good as It Gets*
C) *Five Easy Pieces*
D) *Easy Rider*

289. What is Alison Krauss's primary instrument?
A) Acoustic bass
B) Banjo
C) Fiddle
D) Guitar

290. Who sang the #1 hits "I'll Try," "Someday," and "Dallas"?
A) Tracy Byrd
B) Alan Jackson
C) Tracy Lawrence
D) Little Texas

291. Who reached the top spot on the country singles charts with the songs "Ready for the Times to Get Better," "Talking in Your Sleep," and "Why Have You Left the One You Left Me For"?
A) Dave & Sugar
B) Crystal Gayle
C) Juice Newton
D) Margo Smith

Answers begin on page 62.

292. Which of these singers has not been married to Lorrie Morgan?

A) Clint Black   C) Jon Randall
B) Sammy Kershaw   D) Keith Whitley

293. What country act had a #1 hit in 1979 with "If I Said You Had a Beautiful Body, Would You Hold It against Me?"

A) Moe Bandy   C) John Conlee
B) Bellamy Brothers   D) Conway Twitty

294. What singer's career has spanned more than 20 years and included the hit singles "You Can Dream of Me," "Some Fools Never Learn," and "Holes in the Floor of Heaven"?

A) John Anderson   C) George Strait
B) Ricky Skaggs   D) Steve Wariner

Lorrie Morgan

295. Who produced George Jones's "He Stopped Loving Her Today," Tammy Wynette's "Stand by Your Man," and Charlie Rich's "The Most Beautiful Girl in the World"?

A) Chet Atkins   B) Bob Ferguson   C) Billy Sherrill   D) Shelby Singleton

296. What Southern fiction writer's name was used as the title for a 1995 Top Ten hit for Rick Treviño?

A) Kaye Gibbons   B) Bobbie Ann Mason   C) Ann Rivers Siddons   D) Michael Lee West

297. What r&b vocal group recorded covers of John Michael Montgomery's hits "I Can Love You like That" and "I Swear"?

A) All-4-One   B) Boyz II Men   C) Color Me Badd   D) Take 6

298. Who began his producing career with Alicia Bridges's disco smash "I Love the Night Life" but went on to produce albums of Dolly Parton, Ricky Van Shelton, Mary Chapin Carpenter, Ricky Skaggs, and Tammy Wynette?

A) Steve Buckingham   C) James Stroud
B) Buddy Cannon   D) Chip Young

299. In what Tim Robbins movie did Kelly Willis appear as an earnest folksinger?

A) *Bob Roberts*   B) *Bull Durham*   C) *Cadillac Man*   D) *Jacob's Ladder*

Answers begin on page 62.

300. **What country group, most popular during the late 1980s, included former members of rock bands Creedence Clearwater Revival and the Doobie Brothers?**
A) Bandana   B) Canyon   C) Highway 101   D) Southern Pacific

301. **Who climbed to the top of the country charts with hits like "Heartbroke," "Highway 40 Blues," and "Country Boy"?**
A) Dan Seals   B) Ricky Van Shelton   C) Ricky Skaggs   D) George Strait

302. **What country group hit #1 with its first single, "Meet in the Middle"?**
A) Confederate Railroad   C) McBride & the Ride
B) Diamond Rio   D) Little Texas

303. **What singer's hits include "My List," "I'm Just Talkin' about Tonight," and "You Shouldn't Kiss Me like This"?**
A) Kenny Chesney   B) Toby Keith   C) Tim McGraw   D) Keith Urban

304. **Who's the oldest member of Lonestar?**
A) Michael Britt   B) Richie McDonald   C) Keech Rainwater   D) Dean Sams

305. **What singer's chart-topping hits include "A Perfect World," "Thinkin' about You," and "Believe Me Baby (I Lied)"?**
A) Deborah Allen   B) Martina McBride   C) Pam Tillis   D) Trisha Yearwood

306. **What singer survived the midair collision of two planes over Texas in 1980?**
A) Cristy Lane   B) Crystal Gayle   C) Charley Pride   D) T.G. Sheppard

307. **Who coined the phrase "Music City" to describe Nashville?**
A) Roy Acuff   B) David Cobb   C) Ralph Emery   D) Red Foley

308. **Which duo has the most #1 hits?**
A) Brooks & Dunn   C) The Judds
B) Everly Brothers   D) Conway Twitty & Loretta Lynn

309. **According to a 1975 record by Waylon Jennings, who "is still the king"?**
A) Roy Acuff   B) Elvis Presley   C) Hank Williams   D) Bob Wills

310. **_Urban Cowboy_ was inspired by a non-fiction article in which magazine?**
A) _Country Music_   B) _Esquire_   C) _Life_   D) _Playboy_

Answers begin on page 62.

311. Before making his name as a producer and record label executive, what instrument did James Stroud play on albums for Eddie Rabbitt, Randy Travis, and others?
A) Bass   B) Drums   C) Guitar   D) Piano

312. What was the name of George Strait's country star character in the 1992 movie *Pure Country*?
A) Dusty Chandler   B) Dusty Rhodes   C) Whitey Shafer   D) Dean Dillon

313. What singer hit the charts during the late 1970s and early 1980s with such records as "Love in the Hot Afternoon," "Farewell Party," and "Fourteen Carat Mind"?
A) John Conlee   B) Earl Thomas Conley   C) Mel Street   D) Gene Watson

314. What singer-songwriter penned Jo Dee Messina's "Bye Bye" and Alan Jackson's "Right on the Money" before finding performing success with "Carlene" and "Just Another Day in Paradise"?
A) Chris Cagle   B) Mark McGuinn   C) Brad Paisley   D) Phil Vassar

315. What singer had #1 hits with "Diggin' Up Bones," "Too Gone Too Long," and "Deeper Than the Holler"?
A) Clint Black   B) Alan Jackson   C) Randy Travis   D) Travis Tritt

316. What singer topped the charts with "Help Me Hold On," "Anymore," and "Can I Trust You with My Heart?"
A) Mark Chesnutt   B) Neal McCoy   C) Randy Travis   D) Travis Tritt

317. What singer had #1 singles with "Love, Me," "In This Life," and "My Kind of Girl"?
A) Billy Dean   B) Hal Ketchum   C) Collin Raye   D) Doug Stone

318. What singer's #1 hits include "Home," "Pickup Man," and "Bigger Than the Beatles"?
A) Mark Collie   B) Billy Dean   C) Joe Diffie   D) Aaron Tippin

319. What pop singer penned the Kenny Rogers-Sheena Easton duet "We've Got Tonight"?
A) Billy Joel   B) Elton John   C) Leo Sayer   D) Bob Seger

320. What singer died after suffering a stomach aneurysm while traveling from a show in Branson, Missouri, to Nashville's Fan Fair?
A) Conway Twitty   B) Dottie West   C) Keith Whitley   D) Faron Young

Answers begin on page 62.

321. To what did Douglas Jackson Brooks change his name, reportedly to avoid confusion with Garth Brooks and Brooks & Dunn's Kix Brooks?

A) Doug Stone   B) Doug Supernaw   C) Jack Ingram   D) Jack Robertson

322. What female singer often performed at Tootsie's before signing her record deal?

A) Terri Clark   B) Faith Hill   C) Reba McEntire   D) LeAnn Rimes

323. What country singer, along with writer J.P. Richardson ("the Big Bopper"), provided the whoops and hollers on Johnny Preston's 1959 hit "Running Bear"?

A) Bobby Bare   B) Ferlin Husky   C) Waylon Jennings   D) George Jones

324. What was Bill Monroe's primary instrument?

A) Banjo   B) Fiddle   C) Dobro   D) Mandolin

325. In Roger Miller's 1965 smash "King of the Road," how much do the "rooms to let" cost?

A) Two bits   C) A buck-and-a-half
B) Fifty cents   D) Ten dollars

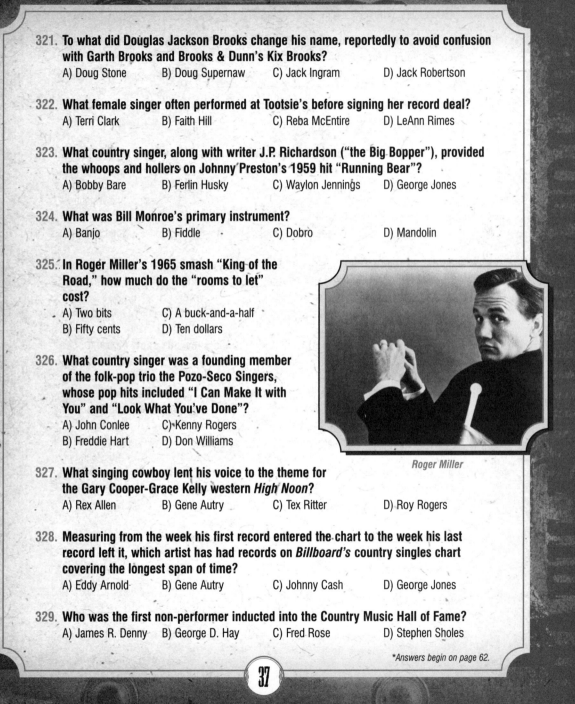

326. What country singer was a founding member of the folk-pop trio the Pozo-Seco Singers, whose pop hits included "I Can Make It with You" and "Look What You've Done"?

A) John Conlee   C) Kenny Rogers
B) Freddie Hart   D) Don Williams

Roger Miller

327. What singing cowboy lent his voice to the theme for the Gary Cooper-Grace Kelly western *High Noon*?

A) Rex Allen   B) Gene Autry   C) Tex Ritter   D) Roy Rogers

328. Measuring from the week his first record entered the chart to the week his last record left it, which artist has had records on *Billboard's* country singles chart covering the longest span of time?

A) Eddy Arnold   B) Gene Autry   C) Johnny Cash   D) George Jones

329. Who was the first non-performer inducted into the Country Music Hall of Fame?

A) James R. Denny   B) George D. Hay   C) Fred Rose   D) Stephen Sholes

Answers begin on page 62.

330. **Who released a rockabilly single called "Hot Dog" under the moniker Corky Jones to avoid damaging his reputation as a country singer?**
   A) Merle Haggard   B) George Jones   C) Buck Owens   D) Johnny Paycheck

331. **Which of these entertainers first hired Roger Miller to play in his or her band?**
   A) Minnie Pearl   B) George Jones   C) Ray Price   D) Faron Young

332. **Before Garth Brooks's *Ropin' the Wind* debuted at #1 in 1991, what was the last country album to top the *Billboard* album chart?**
   A) Johnny Cash, *Johnny Cash at San Quentin*
   B) Glen Campbell, *Wichita Lineman*
   C) Kenny Rogers, *Greatest Hits*
   D) Eric Weissberg & Steve Mandell, "Dueling Banjos" from the Original Soundtrack *Deliverance*

333. **Who owned the rooming house at 620 Boscobel Street in Nashville in which musicians like Carl Smith, Faron Young, and Roger Miller stayed at some point during their careers?**
   A) Louise Hackler   B) Hattie Louise Bess   C) Delia "Mom" Upchurch   D) Marijohn Wilkin

334. **Who was the regular host of ABC-TV's late-1950s television show *Ozark Jubilee*?**
   A) Red Foley   B) Hawkshaw Hawkins   C) Webb Pierce   D) George Morgan

335. **What 1980 movie's soundtrack featured the music of country stars Mickey Gilley, Kenny Rogers, and Johnny Lee, as well as that of countryish pop acts like Jimmy Buffett, Dan Fogelberg, and the Eagles?**
   A) *Bronco Billy*   B) *Honeysuckle Rose*   C) *Roadie*   D) *Urban Cowboy*

336. **What 1980s pop singer appeared in Reba McEntire's "Is There Life Out There?" video?**
   A) Bryan Adams   B) Huey Lewis   C) Robert Palmer   D) Lionel Richie

337. **According to a 1966 hit by Roger Miller, where can't you roller skate?**
   A) In a parakeet cage   C) In a baseball pool
   B) In a buffalo herd   D) In a watermelon patch

338. **What was Travis Tritt's autobiography called?**
   A) *Country Club*   C) *Ten Feet Tall and Bulletproof*
   B) *It's All About to Change*   D) *No Hats*

Answers begin on page 62.

339. **Who brought James Brown to perform at the Grand Ole Opry?**
A) Bill Anderson   B) Jim Ed Brown   C) Stonewall Jackson   D) Porter Wagoner

340. **What singer, after hitting the pop charts with songs like "Down in the Boondocks" and "I Knew You When," switched over to country and hit with such songs as "Tell It Like It Is" and "Love Has No Right"?**
A) Billy Joe Royal   B) Jim Stafford   C) Joe Sun   D) Freddy Weller

341. **What Grand Ole Opry star ran for governor of Tennessee on the Republican ticket in 1948?**
A) Roy Acuff   B) Jimmie Davis   C) Red Foley   D) Uncle Dave Macon

342. **Who supported her younger siblings by singing in a resort after her mother and stepfather were killed in a 1987 car wreck?**
A) Faith Hill   B) Jo Dee Messina   C) Shania Twain   D) Trisha Yearwood

343. **What singer released English, Spanish, and bilingual versions of his debut single, "Just Enough Rope"?**
A) Freddy Fender   B) John Arthur Martinez   C) Johnny Rodriguez   D) Rick Treviño

344. **Four acts topped both the country and pop singles charts in 1975. Which one did it twice?**
A) Glen Campbell   B) John Denver   C) Freddy Fender   D) B.J. Thomas

345. **What singer contracted a voice disorder called spastic dysphonia, nearly ending a promising career that had included such hits as "Undo the Right" and "You Gave Me a Mountain"?**
A) Johnny Bush   B) Johnny Darrell   C) Darrell McCall   D) C.W. McCall

346. **Who played guitar for Tom T. Hall's Storytellers band before topping the charts on his own with "You Always Come Back (to Hurting Me)" and "Ridin' My Thumb to Mexico"?**
A) Freddie Hart   B) Johnny Rodriguez   C) Joe Stampley   D) Nat Stuckey

347. **What singer had recorded both "Cold Day in July" and "Tonight the Heartache's on Me" before the Dixie Chicks?**
A) Gillian Welch   B) Joy Lynn White   C) Lari White   D) Kelly Willis

348. **What was Elvis Presley's first feature film?**
A) *Jailhouse Rock*   B) *King Creole*   C) *Love Me Tender*   D) *Loving You*

Answers begin on page 62.

349. What singer preceded his solo career with memberships in the New Christy Minstrels and the First Edition?

A) Glen Campbell   B) Kris Kristofferson   C) Kenny Rogers   D) Don Williams

350. What was Natalie Maines's first concert appearance with the Dixie Chicks after joining the group?

A) Quaker State Oil Convention
B) Houston Livestock Show and Rodeo
C) Red Steagall's Cowboy Gathering & Western Swing Festival
D) Nashville's Bluebird Café

Dixie Chicks

351. What country singer recorded Coca-Cola's famous "Country Sunshine" jingle of the 1970s?

A) Donna Fargo   C) Dottie West
B) Lynn Anderson   D) Dolly Parton

352. What singer topped the charts in the early 1990s with his first two singles, "What's It to You" and "Live Until I Die"?

A) Tracy Byrd   C) Doug Supernaw
B) Mark Chesnutt   D) Clay Walker

353. Who sings lead for Sawyer Brown?

A) Gregg "Hobie" Hubbard   C) Jim Scholten
B) Mark Miller   D) Joe Smyth

354. If you had walked into the offices of the now-defunct MTM Records during the 1980s, whom might you have seen behind the receptionist's desk?

A) Holly Dunn   B) Martina McBride   C) Judy Rodman   D) Trisha Yearwood

355. Who sings lead for Diamond Rio?

A) Brian Prout   B) Marty Roe   C) Dan Truman   D) Dana Williams

356. Which famed Nashville session pianist was blinded by a knife accident when he was a young child?

A) David Briggs   C) Hargus "Pig" Robbins
B) Marvin Hughes   D) Matt Rollings

Answers begin on page 62.

357. **What Texas-born singer-songwriter penned the Merle Haggard & Willie Nelson hit "Pancho and Lefty" as well as the Don Williams & Emmylou Harris chart-topper "If I Needed You"?**
    A) Guy Clark   B) Mickey Newbury   C) Billy Joe Shaver   D) Townes Van Zandt

358. **What was the famed Nashville nightclub Tootsie's Orchid Lounge called before Hattie Louise "Tootsie" Bess bought it in 1960?**
    A) Louise's   B) Mom's   C) The Orchid   D) Toot's

359. **What honky-tonk piano player had a heart attack onstage in 1962?**
    A) Merrill Moore   B) Moon Mullican   C) Al Stricklin   D) Del Wood

360. **Who produced such classic records as Patsy Cline's "Crazy," Conway Twitty's "Hello Darlin'," and Brenda Lee's "I'm Sorry"?**
    A) Jerry Bradley   B) Owen Bradley   C) Jerry Kennedy   D) Felton Jarvis

361. **What Texas singer-songwriter wrote the chart-topping hits "Angry All the Time," recorded by Tim McGraw, and "Travelin' Soldier," cut by the Dixie Chicks?**
    A) Radney Foster   B) Pat Green   C) Bruce Robison   D) Charlie Robison

362. **For what Disney film did Roger Miller provide the music?**
    A) *Bedknobs and Broomsticks*   C) *The Rescuers*
    B) *Pete's Dragon*   D) *Robin Hood*

363. **What country singer had a role in Billy Bob Thornton's 1996 film *Sling Blade*?**
    A) Jerry Reed   B) Randy Travis   C) Travis Tritt   D) Dwight Yoakam

364. **What sharecropper's son penned the classic country tunes "It Makes No Difference Now," "I Love You So Much It Hurts," and "Slippin' Around"?**
    A) Ted Daffan   B) Red Foley   C) Floyd Tillman   D) Jimmy Wakely

365. **Whose first hit was "Why Baby Why"?**
    A) George Jones   C) Warren Smith & Shirley Collie
    B) Red Sovine & Webb Pierce   D) Hank Locklin

366. **What band's members had previously backed Bob Dylan, Eric Clapton, Leon Russell, and Bonnie Raitt?**
    A) Diamond Rio   B) Ricochet   C) Lonestar   D) The Tractors

*Answers begin on page 62.

367. Who said of Elvis Presley, "His kind of music is deplorable, a rancid smelling aphrodisiac . . . It fosters almost totally negative and destructive reactions in young people"?
A) Dwight D. Eisenhower   C) Hank Snow
B) Richard Nixon   D) Frank Sinatra

368. Which of the Oak Ridge Boys sings bass?
A) Duane Allen   B) Richard Sterban   C) Joe Bonsall   D) William Lee Golden

369. What future country star was just 13 when Lester Flatt hired him as a mandolinist?
A) Vince Gill   B) Ricky Skaggs   C) Marty Stuart   D) Keith Whitley

370. What actor had the lead role in *Urban Cowboy*?
A) Harrison Ford   B) Richard Gere   C) Bill Murray   D) John Travolta

371. Who is the Mavericks' lead vocalist?
A) Raul Malo   B) Robert Reynolds   C) Paul Deakin   D) Nick Kane

372. Who played the piano parts on Charlie Rich's "Behind Closed Doors" and Crystal Gayle's "Don't It Make My Brown Eyes Blue"?
A) David Briggs   C) Hargus "Pig" Robbins
B) Ron Oates   D) Bobby Wood

373. What former gate guard at Elvis Presley's Graceland mansion topped both the country and pop charts in 1974 with "I Can Help"?
A) Kris Kristofferson   B) Ronnie McDowell   C) Billy Swan   D) Tony Joe White

374. What *Playboy* cartoonist penned Johnny Cash's "A Boy Named Sue," Dave & Sugar's "Queen of the Silver Dollar," and Loretta Lynn's "One's on the Way"?
A) Steve Sholes   B) Shel Silverstein   C) Si Siman   D) Shelby Singleton

375. Whom did Marty Stuart marry on July 8, 1997?
A) Rosanne Cash   B) Skeeter Davis   C) Connie Smith   D) Sammi Smith

376. What songwriter-musician penned the Everly Brothers' "Walk Right Back," Keith Whitley's "I'm No Stranger to the Rain," and the theme from *The Mary Tyler Moore Show*?
A) Charlie Black   B) Sonny Curtis   C) Ted Harris   D) Norman Petty

*Answers begin on page 62.

377. Who has been Clint Black's primary co-writer throughout his career?

A) Matraca Berg   B) Skip Ewing   C) Hayden Nicholas   D) Shake Russell

378. Who had her first #1 hit in 1989 with "Timber, I'm Falling in Love"?

A) Suzy Bogguss   C) Patty Loveless
B) Mary Chapin Carpenter   D) Pam Tillis

379. What singer paid clothier Nudie $20,000 to customize a 1962 Pontiac Bonneville with horseshoes, ornamental handguns, silver dollars, and other accessories?

A) Buck Owens   B) Gram Parsons   C) Webb Pierce   D) Elvis Presley

380. What entertainer, though he topped the charts a half-dozen times with songs like "Good Woman Blues" and "Coca Cola Cowboy," is probably better known because of his stutter?

A) Freddie Hart   B) Webb Pierce   C) Cal Smith   D) Mel Tillis

381. What Country Music Hall of Famer's recording career spanned 30 years and included hits like "Singing the Blues," "Don't Worry," and "Devil Woman"?

A) Don Gibson   B) Roger Miller   C) George Morgan   D) Marty Robbins

382. Which Country Music Hall of Fame member saw recordings of "Four Walls," "He'll Have to Go," and "Am I Losing You" cross to the pop charts?

A) Eddy Arnold   C) Jim Reeves
B) Johnny Bond   D) Floyd Tillman

383. What's the name of Willie Nelson's guitar?

A) Apache   C) Pardner
B) Champion   D) Trigger

384. What country-rock group collaborated with such veteran artists as Roy Acuff, Jimmy Martin, Mother Maybelle Carter, Doc Watson, and Earl Scruggs for 1972's historic *Will the Circle Be Unbroken* album?

A) Flying Burrito Brothers   C) New Grass Revival
B) International Submarine Band   D) Nitty Gritty Dirt Band

Webb Pierce

Answers begin on page 62.

385. **Hee Haw began as a summer replacement for what series?**
    A) Rowan & Martin's Laugh-In
    B) The Johnny Cash Show
    C) The Smothers Brothers Comedy Hour
    D) Land of the Giants

386. **Vince Gill was formerly married to a member of which vocal duo?**
    A) Baillie & the Boys
    B) The Judds
    C) Sweethearts of the Rodeo
    D) John & Audrey Wiggins

387. **Richard Thomas, who portrayed Hank Williams Jr. in a 1983 made-for-TV movie, was better known for starring in which 1970s television show?**
    A) Happy Days   B) The Rockford Files   C) Three's Company   D) The Waltons

388. **What singer wrote a western novel called The Small Man?**
    A) Little Jimmy Dickens
    B) Tom T. Hall
    C) Marty Robbins
    D) Porter Wagoner

389. **What songwriting team penned Randy Travis's "On the Other Hand" and "Forever and Ever, Amen," as well as "When You Say Nothing at All"?**
    A) Skip Ewing & Max D. Barnes
    B) Troy Seals & Max D. Barnes
    C) Don Schlitz & Paul Overstreet
    D) Trey Bruce & Russell Smith

390. **Who was Bill Monroe's first banjo player?**
    A) Grandpa Jones   B) Uncle Dave Macon   C) Earl Scruggs   D) Stringbean

391. **Who sang the theme for The Dukes of Hazzard, the CBS television show that aired from 1978 to 1985?**
    A) Jessi Colter   B) Waylon Jennings   C) Bobby Bare   D) Willie Nelson

392. **What singer's career never fully recovered from the effects of a 1950s arrest for possession of marijuana?**
    A) Al Dexter   B) Wayne Raney   C) Wesley Tuttle   D) T. Texas Tyler

393. **What do the call letters "WSM" stand for?**
    A) We Sell Music
    B) We Shield Millions
    C) Where Singles Meet
    D) Where Service Matters

394. **Who is the youngest person to have a charting country record?**
    A) Billy Gilman   B) Brenda Lee   C) LeAnn Rimes   D) Tanya Tucker

Answers begin on page 62.

395. What was George Strait's first album for MCA Records?
A) *Strait Country*
B) *Strait from the Heart*
C) *Right or Wrong*
D) *Something Special*

396. What Nashville producer was once a Los Angeles studio guitarist playing for the likes of Michael Jackson and Madonna?
A) Byron Gallimore
B) Dann Huff
C) David Malloy
D) Paul Worley

397. What was the name of the Tim McGraw/Faith Hill tour during which the couple became romantically involved?
A) McGraw/Hill—Book It!
B) Soul2Soul
C) Spontaneous Combustion
D) The Wild Ones

398. Who made headlines in 1972 for spanking a girl in the audience at his Clarksburg, West Virginia, concert?
A) Buck Owens
B) Webb Pierce
C) Ernest Tubb
D) Faron Young

399. Who is the shortest member of the Country Music Hall of Fame?
A) Little Jimmy Dickens
B) Grandpa Jones
C) Frank "Pee Wee" King
D) Brenda Lee

400. Who recorded the original version of "Walkin' in Memphis," which Lonestar recorded for its 2003 CD, *From There to Here - Greatest Hits*?
A) Marc Almond
B) Marc Anthony
C) Marc Cohn
D) Marc Nelson

401. What action-film star had the lead in *Fire Down Below*, which featured such country stars as Randy Travis, Ed Bruce, Travis Tritt, Mark Collie, Kris Kristofferson, and Marty Stuart?
A) Jackie Chan
B) Clint Eastwood
C) Steven Seagal
D) Jean-Claude Van Damme

402. What songwriter, who has co-written hits for Garth Brooks, Reba McEntire, Joe Diffie, and others, was severely burned in a 1974 industrial electronics fire and required more than 200 surgical procedures?
A) Kent Blazy
B) Richard Fagan
C) Mark D. Sanders
D) Kim Williams

403. In her 1975 hit "I'm Not Lisa," what does Jessi Colter say her name is?
A) Jessi
B) Julie
C) Joni
D) Miriam

*Answers begin on page 62.

404. What television sitcom was Michael Reynolds watching when he came up with the name for the group Pinmonkey?

A) *Friends* B) *Gilligan's Island* C) *Home Improvement* D) *The Simpsons*

405. What bluegrass great hired Ricky Skaggs and Keith Whitley for his band during the early 1970s?

A) Bill Monroe B) Lester Flatt C) Jimmy Martin D) Ralph Stanley

406. Alan Jackson once had a pet named Peanut. What kind of animal was it?

A) Dog B) Raccoon C) Snake D) Spider monkey

407. At what Canadian resort was Shania Twain working when she was discovered by Nashville attorney Dick Frank?

A) Deerhurst Resort
B) Ogopogo Resort
C) Manoir Lac Etchemin
D) Eagle Nest Lodge

408. Which artist put Brad Paisley's "I'm Gonna Miss Her (the Fishing Song)" on hold, leading to Paisley's signing a record deal with Arista Records?

A) Brooks & Dunn C) Lee Roy Parnell
B) Alan Jackson D) Pam Tillis

Shania Twain

409. Who sang the low bass notes on the 1977 Elvis Presley hit "Way Down"?

A) Hugh Jarrett B) Richard Sterban C) J.D. Sumner D) Ray Walker

410. Prior to marrying Tim McGraw, to which top producer was Faith Hill engaged?

A) Tony Brown B) Byron Gallimore C) Scott Hendricks D) Kyle Lehning

411. Who is the only licensed mortician to have a chart-topping country record?

A) Johnny Cash C) Ray Pillow
B) John Conlee D) Kenny Price

412. Who was the first person to autograph Willie Nelson's famed Martin N-20 acoustic guitar?

A) Johnny Bush B) Johnny Cash C) Paul English D) Leon Russell

*Answers begin on page 62.

413. What Myrtle Beach, South Carolina, nightclub was home to Alabama from 1973 to 1980?

A) The Attic   B) The Bowery   C) Anchor Lounge   D) Studebaker's

414. Who was Alabama's original drummer?

A) Mark Herndon   B) Bennett Vartanian   C) Jackie Owen   D) Rick Scott

415. What was the name of Dolly Parton's character in the movie *9 to 5*?

A) Judy Bernley   B) Truvy Jones   C) Violet Newstead   D) Doralee Rhodes

416. Though Patty Loveless's *When Fallen Angels Fly* won the Country Music Association's Album of the Year award in 1995, it originally wasn't even one of the nominees. Which album was disqualified from contention, thereby opening the way for Loveless to win?

A) *Strait Out of the Box*, George Strait
B) *The Hits*, Garth Brooks
C) *Now That I've Found You: A Collection*, Alison Krauss
D) *Healing Hands of Time*, Willie Nelson

417. What was the name of Mary Kay Place's country-singing character on the 1970s sitcom *Mary Hartman, Mary Hartman*?

A) Barbi Bodine   B) Wynette Byrd   C) Loretta Haggers   D) Louise Lasser

418. Which of these names is a pseudonym?

A) Narvel Felts   C) Ferlin Husky
B) Englebert Humperdinck   D) Stonewall Jackson

419. What Kenny Rogers album did members of the pop group the Bee Gees write and produce?

A) *Eyes That See in the Dark*   C) *Love Will Turn You Around*
B) *Heart of the Matter*   D) *What About Me?*

420. What singer was severely injured in a 1984 head-on collision in which the driver of the other car was killed?

A) Barbara Mandrell   C) Dottie West
B) Charly McClain   D) Shelly West

421. Which artist has had charting country singles with the greatest number of duet partners?

A) George Jones   B) Willie Nelson   C) Conway Twitty   D) Tammy Wynette

*Answers begin on page 62.

422. On what country music show was LeAnn Rimes regularly performing when she was signed to Curb Records?
A) *Louisiana Hayride*, Shreveport
B) Grand Ole Opry, Nashville
C) *Big D Jamboree*, Dallas
D) *Johnnie High's Country Music Revue*, Fort Worth

423. What legendary Grand Ole Opry performer had "THANK YOU" written in large letters on the back of his guitar?
A) Bill Carlisle   B) Jimmie Davis   C) Hank Snow   D) Ernest Tubb

424. In what year did *Urban Cowboy* become a box-office smash and "Tennessee River" become Alabama's first #1 hit?
A) 1979   B) 1980   C) 1981   D) 1982

425. In what year did Clint Black, Garth Brooks, and Alan Jackson all release their debut albums?
A) 1986   B) 1988   C) 1989   D) 1990

426. What was Minnie Pearl's trademark greeting?
A) "Hey, y'all!"
B) "How-dee!"
C) "How are ya, how are ya, how are ya?"
D) "Good to see you!"

427. From whom did the Marshall Tucker Band take its name?
A) The group's lead singer
B) The band's high-school gym teacher
C) A local bluesman
D) A blind piano tuner

428. What did Tim McGraw have tattooed on his left thigh to commemorate his first hit, "Indian Outlaw"?
A) A peace sign with a daisy
B) An Indian headdress
C) A single feather
D) A leprechaun

429. What singer released five consecutive chart-topping sides in 1944 and 1945, including "So Long Pal," which spent 13 weeks at #1?
A) Eddy Arnold   B) Ted Daffan   C) Al Dexter   D) Red Foley

430. What singer made his first official Grand Ole Opry appearance the night Garth Brooks was inducted as a member?
A) Mark Collie   B) Joe Diffie   C) Alan Jackson   D) Travis Tritt

Answers begin on page 62.

431. Who has produced all of Garth Brooks's albums except *In the Life of Chris Gaines*?
A) Blake Chancey   B) David Malloy   C) Allen Reynolds   D) Paul Worley

432. What artist was the cover subject of the first *Country Weekly*?
A) Garth Brooks   B) Johnny Cash   C) Billy Ray Cyrus   D) Conway Twitty

433. Who played bass on Roger Miller's 1965 smash "King of the Road"?
A) Lightnin' Chance   B) Junior Huskey   C) Bob Moore   D) Henry Strzelecki

434. What artist was featured on the first issue of *Country Music* magazine?
A) Johnny Cash   B) Merle Haggard   C) Buck Owens   D) Dolly Parton

435. What rock band originally recorded the song "Dixie Chicken," from which the Dixie Chicks took their name?
A) Atlanta Rhythm Section   C) Charlie Daniels Band
B) Barefoot Jerry   D) Little Feat

436. Who was the only member of the 1939 version of Roy Acuff's Smoky Mountain Boys still playing with Acuff at the time of Acuff's death in 1992?
A) Bashful Brother Oswald
B) Howdy Forrester
C) Jimmie Riddle
D) Lonnie Wilson

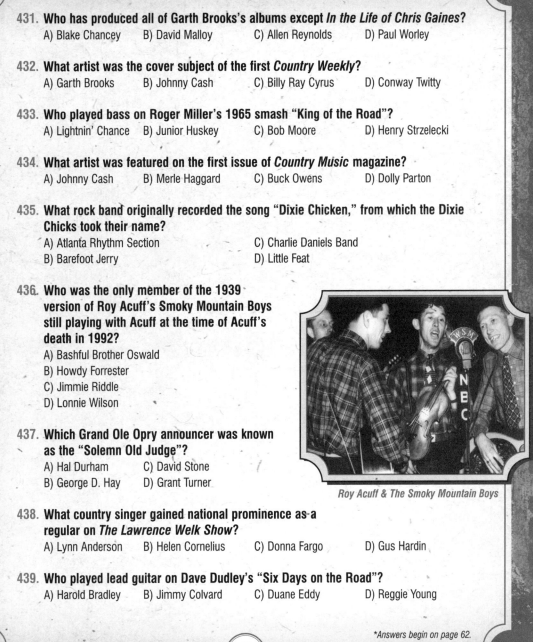

Roy Acuff & The Smoky Mountain Boys

437. Which Grand Ole Opry announcer was known as the "Solemn Old Judge"?
A) Hal Durham   C) David Stone
B) George D. Hay   D) Grant Turner

438. What country singer gained national prominence as a regular on *The Lawrence Welk Show*?
A) Lynn Anderson   B) Helen Cornelius   C) Donna Fargo   D) Gus Hardin

439. Who played lead guitar on Dave Dudley's "Six Days on the Road"?
A) Harold Bradley   B) Jimmy Colvard   C) Duane Eddy   D) Reggie Young

Answers begin on page 62.

440. About which singer did Jerry Chesnut write "T-R-O-U-B-L-E"?
A) Waylon Jennings   B) Wayne Kemp   C) Elvis Presley   D) Little David Wilkins

441. What singer worked as an assistant in a mortuary before becoming a country star?
A) Eddy Arnold   B) Joe Nichols   C) Ernest Tubb   D) Gene Watson

442. What did Lyle Lovett originally intend as the title for his *I Love Everybody* album?
A) *Creeps Like Me*   B) *Lovett or Leave It*   C) *Fat Babies*   D) *Lyle, Lyle Crocodile*

443. A member of which group starred as Paul McCartney in a Broadway production of *Beatlemania*?
A) Baillie & the Boys   B) Desert Rose Band   C) Foster & Lloyd   D) Highway 101

444. What singer was once in a band called Sandu Scott & the Scotties that also included two members—Dino Danelli and Felix Cavaliere—who would go on to form the Young Rascals?
A) Kenny Dale   B) Lee Greenwood   C) Gary Morris   D) B.J. Thomas

445. What member of the *Hee Haw* cast wrote the show's theme song?
A) Archie Campbell   B) Roy Clark   C) Grandpa Jones   D) Sheb Wooley

446. What's the name of the Tennessee town that Loretta Lynn and her husband purchased and made their home?
A) Bellbuckle   B) Butcher Holler   C) Grinder's Switch   D) Hurricane Mills

447. Where was the Stateside Club Mel Tillis sang about in his 1966 hit "Stateside"?
A) Tampa, Florida   C) Hendersonville, Tennessee
B) Berlin, West Germany   D) Okinawa, Japan

448. What television show is the bartender watching in Tom T. Hall's "(Old Dogs, Children and) Watermelon Wine"?
A) *Bonanza*   B) *Gunsmoke*   C) *Ironside*   D) *Mannix*

449. What injury-prone singer had her cheekbone fractured during a celebrity softball game, dislocated her shoulder when a fan nearly pulled her out of a convertible, and broke her left hand in a motorcycle accident?
A) Deana Carter   B) Terri Clark   C) Jo Dee Messina   D) Lorrie Morgan

Answers begin on page 62.

450. Which singer played Pippa McKenna on the 1980s television sitcom *The Facts of Life*?

    A) Sherrié Austin   B) Sara Evans   C) Jamie O'Neal   D) Chely Wright

451. Which of these women is not one that Johnny Cash claims wants him in his version of Bob Dylan's "Wanted Man"?

    A) Lucy Watson   B) Nelly Johnson   C) Jeannie Brown   D) Becky Thatcher

452. What singer worked as a beautician before moving to Nashville in 1966—then kept her license current, just in case her records ever stopped selling?

    A) Lynn Anderson   B) Penny DeHaven   C) Jeannie Seely   D) Tammy Wynette

453. What songwriter lost some of his fingers in a sawmill accident before becoming a songwriter and writing such songs as John Anderson's "I'm Just an Old Chunk of Coal (but I'm Gonna Be a Diamond Some Day)" and Bobby Bare's "Ride Me Down Easy"?

    A) Bobby Braddock   B) Bob McDill   C) Curley Putman   D) Billy Joe Shaver

454. What star began her career in the Nashville music industry by selling T-shirts at Fan Fair?

    A) Faith Hill   B) Martina McBride   C) Jo Dee Messina   D) Trisha Yearwood

455. Which Exile member had a father who was an announcer on *Renfro Valley Barn Dance,* and a mother who was a member of the Coon Creek Girls stringband?

    A) Marlon Hargis   B) Sonny LeMaire   C) J.P. Pennington   D) Les Taylor

456. Who produced the two singles Randy Travis recorded for Paula Records under the name Randy Traywick?

    A) Dickey Lee   B) Tommy Overstreet   C) Joe Stampley   D) Joe Sun

457. Which of these performers has a sibling in the duo Montgomery Gentry?

    A) Bobbie Gentry   C) John Michael Montgomery

    B) Alabama's Teddy Gentry   D) Melba Montgomery

458. What member of Lonestar left the group in 1998?

    A) Michael Britt   B) Richie McDonald   C) John Rich   D) Dean Sams

459. Lonestar drummer Keech Rainwater and bassist Michael Britt previously played in which band, which had one Top Forty hit with "Hot Nights" in 1989?

    A) Atlanta   B) Bandana   C) Canyon   D) Dixiana

Answers begin on page 62.

460. **For which company did Sammy Kershaw once work as a construction supervisor?**
A) Home Depot   B) Lowe's   C) K-mart   D) Wal-Mart

461. **In what Tennessee city did Ralph Peer first record Jimmie Rodgers and the Carter Family, in the summer of 1927?**
A) Bristol   B) Knoxville   C) Johnson City   D) Nashville

462. **At what Austin, Texas, nightclub did both Hank Williams and Johnny Horton make their final public performances?**
A) The Continental Club
B) The Austin Opera House
C) Liberty Lunch
D) The Skyline

The Carter Family

463. **What singer sang backup for country-rock pioneer Gram Parsons before going solo?**
A) Emmylou Harris   C) Linda Ronstadt
B) Juice Newton   D) Margo Smith

464. **After whose great-great-grandfather is Klein, Texas, named?**
A) Tracy Byrd   C) Lyle Lovett
B) Patsy Cline   D) George Strait

465. **What magazine employed cartoonist Jack Davis, who designed such 1960s album covers as Johnny Cash's *Everybody Loves a Nut*, Jerry Reed's *The Uptown Poker Club*, and Little Jimmy Dickens's *May the Bird of Paradise Fly Up Your Nose*?**
A) *Esquire*   B) *Life*   C) *Mad*   D) *The New Yorker*

466. **What band, using the pseudonym the Toots Uncommon, backed comedian Steve Martin on his 1978 novelty hit "King Tut"?**
A) Asleep at the Wheel   C) Nitty Gritty Dirt Band
B) Exile   D) Earl Scruggs Revue

467. **What future country star played fiddle on Bob Dylan's *Nashville Skyline* album?**
A) Charlie Daniels   C) Michael Martin Murphey
B) Barbara Mandrell   D) John Wesley Ryles

Answers begin on page 62.

468. **What singer modeled for the Minnie Pearl statue that now sits in Nashville's Ryman Auditorium?**

A) Terri Clark   B) Chely Wright   C) Michelle Wright   D) Trisha Yearwood

469. **BlackHawk's Henry Paul was a founding member of which southern rock group?**

A) .38 Special   C) Molly Hatchet
B) Marshall Tucker Band   D) The Outlaws

470. **Where is the King's Record Shop pictured on the cover of the Rosanne Cash album of the same name?**

A) Goodlettsville, Tennessee   C) Montgomery, Alabama
B) Louisville, Kentucky   D) Buffalo, New York

471. **Who played fiddle on Alabama's "If You're Gonna Play in Texas (You Gotta Have a Fiddle in the Band)"?**

A) Jeff Cook   B) Johnny Gimble   C) Mark O'Connor   D) Blaine Sprouse

472. **Which group recorded an album under the pseudonym Lester "Roadhog" Moran & His Cadillac Cowboys?**

A) Alabama   C) Oak Ridge Boys
B) Nitty Gritty Dirt Band   D) Statler Brothers

473. **What was the first album to debut in the #1 position on *Billboard's* country chart?**

A) *No Fences*, Garth Brooks   C) *Old 8x10*, Randy Travis
B) *Ocean Front Property*, George Strait   D) *Greatest Hits*, Kenny Rogers

474. **What position did Charley Pride play for the Memphis Red Sox of the Negro American League?**

A) Catcher   B) First base   C) Pitcher   D) Outfield

475. **In which of these films did Conway Twitty not appear?**

A) *College Confidential*   C) *Platinum High School*
B) *The Girl Can't Help It*   D) *Sex Kittens Go to College*

476. **In which subject did Mary Chapin Carpenter receive her bachelor of arts degree from Brown University in 1981?**

A) American civilization   C) Political science
B) English literature   D) Music

Answers begin on page 62.

477. What's the name of the duck in Ricky Van Shelton's series of children's books?

A) Duck Duck   B) Honker   C) Quacker   D) Ricky

478. Which of these singers played pro basketball?

A) Alabama's Randy Owen   C) Restless Heart's Larry Stewart

B) Diamond Rio's Marty Roe   D) Sawyer Brown's Mark Miller

479. What renowned movie director made a cameo appearance in the video for the Reba McEntire-Linda Davis duet "Does He Love You"?

A) Francis Ford Coppola   C) Rob Reiner

B) John Hughes   D) Martin Scorsese

480. At what Nashville nightclub did Randy Travis cook and wash dishes before signing his record deal?

A) Legends Corner   C) Robert's Western World

B) Nashville Palace   D) The Sutler

481. What future country star began playing bass for Dottie West at age 17?

A) John Conlee   B) Larry Gatlin   C) Ronnie McDowell   D) Steve Wariner

482. Which singer worked as a physical education instructor in Canada?

A) Terri Clark   B) Anne Murray   C) Shania Twain   D) Michelle Wright

483. Who designed the infamous red dress that Reba McEntire wore to the 1993 Country Music Association awards ceremony?

A) Bob Mackie   B) Manuel   C) Sherry McCoy   D) Sandi Spika

484. Under what name did George Jones record rockabilly sides for Starday Records?

A) Commonwealth Jones   C) Smith 'n' Jones

B) Corky Jones   D) Thumper Jones

485. For what company did Elvis Presley make his sole television commercial?

A) Lansky's Clothing Store   C) Southern Doughnuts

B) Schwab's Dry Goods Store   D) Sun Studios

486. Which band got their recording contract—and $100,000—by winning television's *Star Search* talent contest in 1983?

A) Bandana   B) Exile   C) Southern Pacific   D) Sawyer Brown

*Answers begin on page 62.

487. What television game show did Tennessee Ernie Ford host?
A) *The Art Ford Show*
B) *College of Musical Knowledge*
C) *Stop the Music*
D) *Truth or Consequences*

488. What Broadway musical had a character named Conrad Birdie that parodied Conway Twitty?
A) *Bye Bye Birdie*
B) *Do Re Mi*
C) *Gypsy*
D) *Once Upon a Mattress*

489. What duo did Ralph Emery dub the "Soap Sisters" on his morning television show because he couldn't remember how to pronounce their names?
A) Davis Sisters
B) The Judds
C) Kinleys
D) Sweethearts of the Rodeo

Conway Twitty

490. Which sister act helped the Bellamy Brothers top the charts in 1986 with "Too Much Is Not Enough"?
A) Forester Sisters
B) Kinleys
C) McCarters
D) Sweethearts of the Rodeo

491. What country supergroup consisted of Johnny Cash, Waylon Jennings, Kris Kristofferson, and Willie Nelson?
A) The Cactus Choir
B) The Highwaymen
C) The Outlaws
D) Wild Choir

492. Which member of the Sons of the Pioneers went on to play Festus Haggen on the television drama *Gunsmoke*?
A) Ken Curtis
B) Bob Nolan
C) Tim Spencer
D) Lloyd Perryman

493. What singer had songs like "Baby Don't Get Hooked on Me" and "Stop and Smell the Roses" reach both the country and the pop charts during the 1970s?
A) Jimmie Davis
B) Mac Davis
C) Paul Davis
D) Skeeter Davis

494. What act spun off from the Kentucky HeadHunters, placing such singles as "Let Go" and "Were You Really Livin'" on the country charts?
A) Almost Brothers
B) Brother Phelps
C) Marcy Brothers
D) Thompson Brothers Band

*Answers begin on page 62.

495. Which singer had five consecutive gold singles during the 1970s, among them "Let Me Be There" and "If You Love Me (Let Me Know)"?

A) Lynn Anderson   B) Crystal Gayle   C) Olivia Newton-John   D) Dolly Parton

496. Who placed "Annie's Song," "Sweet Surrender," and "Back Home Again" on both the country and pop charts during the 1970s?

A) Lynn Anderson   B) John Denver   C) Tom T. Hall   D) Olivia Newton-John

497. What Country Music Hall of Famer's singles include "Faded Love," "When I Get Thru with You (You'll Love Me, Too)," and "Walkin' after Midnight"?

A) Patsy Cline   B) Don Gibson   C) Floyd Tillman   D) Bob Wills

498. Which member of BlackHawk died of cancer in 2002?

A) Henry Paul   B) Dave Robbins   C) Van Stephenson   D) Randy Threet

499. Who placed two novelty records—"Cuzz Yore So Sweet" and "Country Music Is Here to Stay"—in the Top Five during the 1950s under the pseudonym Simon Crum?

A) Johnny Bond   B) Ferlin Husky   C) Conway Twitty   D) Slim Whitman

500. Which country singer found pop success with the novelty songs "Dang Me," "Chug-a-Lug," and "Do-Wacka-Do"?

A) Johnny Bond   B) Grandpa Jones   C) Roger Miller   D) Red Sovine

501. Who had a Top Ten hit in 1982 with the song "16th Avenue"?

A) Deborah Allen   B) Lacy J. Dalton   C) Terri Gibbs   D) Becky Hobbs

502. Which artist had to have surgery in 1994 to drain a cyst in his brain – the same month he had his first #1 single, "Your Love Amazes Me"?

A) John Berry   C) Neal McCoy
B) Billy Dean   D) John Michael Montgomery

503. Which country singer got his or her stage name from a national fast-food chain?

A) Crystal Gayle   B) Claude King   C) Juice Newton   D) Roy Rogers

504. What country-rock group recorded the album that gave Sweethearts of the Rodeo their name?

A) Byrds   C) Flying Burrito Brothers
B) Eagles   D) Poco

*Answers begin on page 62.

505. How did Kix Brooks get his nickname?
A) From being an all-state place-kicker on his high school football team
B) From being kicked by a mule as an 8-year-old and spending two weeks in the hospital
C) From kicking his mother while he was in the womb
D) From a bad habit he picked up as a toddler

506. Which female country singer has the most #1 hits?
A) Crystal Gayle   B) Reba McEntire   C) Dolly Parton   D) Tammy Wynette

507. How much did Willie Nelson end up paying the Internal Revenue Service to settle his tax debt?
A) $650,000   B) $3.2 million   C) $10.1 million   D) $16.7 million

508. Who was the first country star to win an Emmy?
A) Garth Brooks   B) Johnny Cash   C) Reba McEntire   D) Hank Williams Jr.

509. Which of these names was not one under which Collin Raye had a charting country record?
A) Collin Raye   B) Collin Wray   C) The Wrays   D) The Wray Brothers Band

510. Under what pseudonym did Sheb Wooley release such novelty records as "Don't Go Near the Eskimos," "Almost Persuaded No. 2," and "Fifteen Beers Ago"?
A) Johnny Bond   B) Ben Colder   C) Lonzo & Oscar   D) The Wooley Mammoth

511. Which producer—also known for his work with rock bands Def Leppard, AC/DC, and the Cars—did Shania Twain marry in 1993?
A) Steve Albini   C) Robert John "Mutt" Lange
B) Roy Thomas Baker   D) Rick Rubin

512. Under what pseudonym did Hank Williams Jr. record such singles as "Custody," "It Don't Take but One Mistake," and "I Was with Red Foley (the Night He Passed Away)"?
A) Bocephus   B) Lonesome Hank   C) Luke the Drifter Jr.   D) Hank Randall

513. These four singers had Top Five hits with "Candy Kisses" in 1949. Whose version went all the way to #1?
A) Elton Britt   B) Cowboy Copas   C) Red Foley   D) George Morgan

514. What animal does Keith Urban have tattooed on his left shoulder?
A) Bull   B) Eagle   C) Koala   D) Snake

*Answers begin on page 62.

515. Which singer released 1961's *Live at the Golden Nugget*, one of country music's first live albums?

A) Eddy Arnold   B) Webb Pierce   C) Jim Reeves   D) Hank Thompson

516. Which singer, as a teen, broke several facial bones (in a car accident) requiring years of reconstructive surgery?

A) Suzy Bogguss   B) Patty Loveless   C) Lorrie Morgan   D) Pam Tillis

517. Which country singer did Hank Williams's widow, Billie Jean Jones Eshliman, marry after Williams's death?

A) Johnny Horton   B) Webb Pierce   C) Ray Price   D) Faron Young

518. What artist was the last entertainer to perform at the Grand Ole Opry's final Ryman Auditorium show in 1974 and the first one to perform at the new Grand Ole Opry House?

A) Roy Acuff   B) Minnie Pearl   C) Marty Robbins   D) Porter Wagoner

Ryman Auditorium

519. Dolly Parton hit the top of the charts in 1981 with "But You Know I Love You." Who had the original hit version, back in 1969?

A) Bill Anderson   C) Conway Twitty
B) Henson Cargill   D) Porter Wagoner

520. When Garth Brooks cut "Callin' Baton Rouge," he had the group who recorded the 1989 hit version of the song record it with him. What was that group?

A) New Grass Revival
B) Oak Ridge Boys
C) Restless Heart
D) Shenandoah

521. Which singing cowboy wrote the Christmas standard "Here Comes Santa Claus (down Santa Claus Lane)"?

A) Rex Allen   B) Gene Autry   C) Roy Rogers   D) Tex Ritter

522. Which singer topped the charts three times in 1981—first with "I Keep Coming Back," then with "Friends" and "Midnight Hauler"?

A) Razzy Bailey   B) Moe Bandy   C) Lee Greenwood   D) Ronnie Milsap

Answers begin on page 62.

523. Which singer topped the charts in the 1980s with hits like "Hell and High Water," "Don't Go to Strangers," and "Darlene"—and also recorded jingles for McDonald's and Taco Bell?
    A) Jim Ed Brown   B) T. Graham Brown   C) Ed Bruce   D) T.G. Sheppard

524. Who won the Country Music Association's first Horizon Award, given in 1980?
    A) John Anderson   B) Rosanne Cash   C) Terri Gibbs   D) T.G. Sheppard

525. Which Pro Football Hall of Fame quarterback won a Super Bowl and had a country hit with his rendition of Hank Williams's "I'm So Lonesome I Could Cry" in the same year?
    A) Terry Bradshaw   B) Joe Namath   C) Roger Staubach   D) Johnny Unitas

526. Which singer topped the country charts during the 1990s with hits like "Brother Jukebox," "I'll Think of Something," "It Sure Is Monday," and "Almost Goodbye"?
    A) Tracy Byrd   B) Mark Chesnutt   C) Joe Diffie   D) Doug Stone

527. Which pop act has not had a Top Forty country hit?
    A) Bee Gees   B) Eric Clapton   C) Billy Joel   D) Pointer Sisters

528. Which country singer served two terms as the governor of Louisiana?
    A) Ted Daffan   B) Jimmie Davis   C) Claude King   D) Al Terry

529. Which of these duos was also husband and wife?
    A) Jim Ed Brown & Helen Cornelius   C) George Jones & Tammy Wynette
    B) Conway Twitty & Loretta Lynn   D) David Frizzell & Shelly West

530. Who did Dolly Parton replace on the *Porter Wagoner Show*?
    A) Liz Anderson   B) Margie Bowes   C) Norma Jean   D) Billie Jo Spears

531. Buck Owens took "Above and Beyond" to #3 in 1960. Who had a #1 hit with the song 29 years later?
    A) Rodney Crowell   B) Ricky Van Shelton   C) Steve Wariner   D) Dwight Yoakam

532. Before Conway Twitty, Loretta Lynn had another duet partner, with whom she recorded such hits as "Mr. and Mrs. Used to Be" and "Who's Gonna Take the Garbage Out." Who was he?
    A) George Jones   B) Ernest Tubb   C) Porter Wagoner   D) Doyle Wilburn

Answers begin on page 62.

533. What real-life railroad disaster inspired the song "The Wreck of the Old '97"?
A) 1903 wreck of Southern Railways Engine 1102 near Danville, Virginia.
B) 1906 head-on collision of two Southern Railroad trains in New Market, Tennessee.
C) 1917 collision in Shepherdsville, Kentucky, that killed 48.
D) April 1900 wreck near Canton, Mississippi.

534. At what address did "Teddy Bear" live, in the 1976 Red Sovine hit of that name?
A) 521 Jefferson Avenue
B) 229 Jackson Street
C) 824 Baker Street
D) 1109 Brookemeade Drive

535. Both Merle Haggard and his song "Mama Tried" appeared in the 1968 film *Killers Three*. What role did Haggard play in the film?
A) Cop
B) Jailer
C) Killer
D) Murder victim

536. Charley Pride's first Grammys came in what field?
A) Country
B) Gospel
C) Pop
D) Rhythm & Blues

537. What act has placed the most Christmas singles on the *Billboard* country charts?
A) Alabama
B) Gene Autry
C) Garth Brooks
D) George Strait

538. Excluding Christmas hits, reissues, B-sides, and duets, which act has had the most consecutive #1 singles?
A) Alabama
B) Earl Thomas Conley
C) Sonny James
D) Buck Owens

539. From which movie did Faron Young get his nickname, "The Young Sheriff"?
A) *Country Music Holiday*
B) *Daniel Boone, Trail Blazer*
C) *Hidden Guns*
D) *Raiders of Old California*

540. George Jones and Tammy Wynette announced their marriage on August 22, 1968. When did they actually get married?
A) May 5, 1968
B) August 21, 1968
C) August 22, 1968
D) February 16, 1969

541. Glen Campbell co-starred in which John Wayne film?
A) *McQ*
B) *Rooster Cogburn*
C) *The Shootist*
D) *True Grit*

542. In "I Love," what drinks does Tom T. Hall say he loves?
A) Beer & milk
B) Coffee & bourbon
C) Coca-Cola & whiskey
D) Scotch & soda

Answers begin on page 62.

543. Who co-wrote lyrics with Skeeter Davis for the Floyd Cramer instrumental "Last Date"?

A) Chet Atkins B) Boudleaux Bryant C) Ralph Emery D) Marijohn Wilkin

544. In August 1957, Merle Haggard and a friend were arrested for trying to burglarize a restaurant. Why did they get caught?

A) They accidentally locked themselves inside.

B) They cleaned out the bar, got drunk, and passed out in the back alley.

C) One of them dropped his wallet, with a driver's license inside.

D) The restaurant was still open.

545. In what Robert Redford film did Freddy Fender have a part?

A) *Brubaker* C) *The Electric Horseman*

B) *The Milagro Beanfield War* D) *The Horse Whisperer*

546. What act has had the most charting *Billboard* country singles without ever reaching the Top Forty?

A) Maury Finny C) Orion

B) Marshall Tucker Band D) Billy Parker

547. Chet Atkins and Kenny Chesney both hail from which eastern Tennessee town?

A) Corryton C) Maryville

B) Luttrell D) Maynardville

Chet Atkins

548. What artist, who would have several hits of his own in the 1970s, wrote Carl Smith's "Loose Talk," Porter Wagoner's "Skid Row Joe," and George Jones's "My Tears Are Overdue"?

A) Johnny Duncan C) Freddie Hart

B) Tom T. Hall D) Earl Thomas Conley

549. What Charley Pride single did RCA Records ship without a promotional photo, in hopes that DJs would listen to the record before noticing the color of Pride's skin?

A) "Does My Ring Hurt Your Finger" C) "Just between You and Me"

B) "I Know One" D) "The Snakes Crawl at Night"

Answers begin on page 62.

⤝ TRIVIA QUIZ ANSWERS ⤞

1. D) Schiff
2. B) Floyd Cramer
3. A) Gene Johnson
4. B) *Diamonds and Dirt*, Rodney Crowell—*Diamonds and Dirt* included these hits: "It's Such a Small World," "She's Crazy for Leavin'," "I Couldn't Leave You If I Tried," "Above and Beyond" and "After All This Time."
5. A) T. Tommy Cutrer
6. B) Vernon Dalhart
7. A) Nashville Brass
8. D) Mac Davis
9. B) Skeeter Davis
10. B) Jimmy Day
11. B) Alton Delmore
12. C) Johnnie & Jack—Jack Anglin died March 7, 1963; Johnnie Wright continued as a solo act, scoring the #1 hit "Hello Vietnam" in 1965.
13. C) Michael Johnson
14. C) He set it afire.
15. D) Lonestar
16. B) Brooks & Dunn
17. B) Martina McBride
18. C) George Strait
19. C) Shania Twain
20. C) *Thank Heavens for Dale Evans*—The Dixie Chicks put out three albums before Natalie Maines joined and the group signed to Monument Records, which released *Wide Open Spaces* in January 1998. *Thank Heavens for Dale Evans* came out in 1990, followed by *Little Ol' Cowgirl* in 1992 and *Shouldn't a Told You That* in 1993.
21. D) Ringo Starr—Starr and Owens remade "Act Naturally" and took it to # 27 in 1989. Starr sang lead on the Beatles' cover of Owens's country smash, taking it to #47 on the pop charts in 1965.
22. C) Steve Sanders—Sanders sang with the quartet from 1987 until Golden rejoined the group in 1996.
23. D) Cajun—Newman's real middle name is Yeve.

24. B) Lyle Lovett—Lovett and Roberts married June 26, 1993, after meeting during the filming of Robert Altman's *The Player*; they divorced in 1996.

25. C) *Beyond the Doll of Cutey*—Not exactly a country album, *Beyond the Doll of Cutey* was released by Warner Bros. in 1983—six years before Tillis's breakout album, *Put Yourself in My Place*.

26. C) Anne Murray—Murray performed on the show's ninth episode, which first aired January 10, 1976. She was also the first country singer to earn a return performance, appearing again on the 102d episode, which was broadcast April 12, 1980.

27. C) Laura Lynch—Lynch and Robin Lynn Macy both sang with the Dixie Chicks pre-Natalie Maines, but Maines replaced Lynch.

28. D) Conway Twitty

29. A) Jean Shepard

30. C) Sissy Spacek

31. B) Eddy Arnold

32. A) Blue Grass Boys

33. A) Billy Ray Cyrus

34. A) Johnny Cash—Johnny Cash was inducted into the Country Music Hall of Fame in 1980 and the Rock and Roll Hall of Fame in 1992. Though Elvis Presley and the Everlys were part of the Rock Hall's first induction class in 1986, they didn't join the ranks of Country Music Hall of Famers until 2001.

35. A) *Reba*

36. D) Ricky Skaggs

37. B) Loretta Lynn

38. A) Banjo

39. B) Billie Joe McAllister

40. D) LeAnn Rimes

41. A) Loretta Lynn—Lynn entered the Hall of Fame in 1988.

42. A) Canton, Ohio—Williams was pronounced dead January 1, 1953, in Oak Hill. He was being chauffeured to Canton for a show there that night.

43. A) Alabama

44. C) Kingston Trio—The Kingston Trio's "Tom Dooley" won the 1958 Grammy for Best Country & Western Performance.

45. A) Roy Acuff
46. D) George Jones
47. D) Accordion
48. B) Dizzy Dean—Dean was a pitcher for the St. Louis Cardinals.
49. C) Hickory Records
50. B) Merle Haggard
51. A) Duncan Cameron
52. A) Bill Anderson
53. B) Dillards
54. C) Cadillac
55. D) Robert Reynolds
56. D) Montgomery Gentry
57. C) Alan Jackson's *Here in the Real World*
58. B) Eddy Arnold—Arnold was elected to the Hall of Fame in 1966; he won the CMA's Entertainer of the Year award the following year.
59. C) Willie Nelson
60. C) 1972—The first Fan Fair was held at Nashville's Municipal Auditorium and drew 5,000 fans.
61. B) Bakersfield
62. C) Possum Hunters
63. C) Mark Herndon—Herndon is from Springfield, Massachusetts, and was hired in 1979, after the other three members had been together for about a decade. Coincidentally, he's also the youngest member of the group.
64. C) Chris Gaines
65. A) Barbi Benton—Benton appeared on the July 1969, March 1970, May 1972, and December 1985 issues of the magazine.
66. C) Bluebird Café
67. C) Diamond Rio—"Meet in the Middle" reached the top of the chart in the June 1, 1991 issue of *Billboard*.
68. A) Dizzy Dean
69. A) Brown's Ferry Four—The group began singing on WLW in Cincinnati in 1943. Future members included Red Foley and Clyde Moody.

70. A) Desert Rose Band
71. A) Bullet Records
72. D) *Wanted: The Outlaws*—Released by RCA in 1976, *Wanted: The Outlaws* contained cuts by Waylon Jennings, Willie Nelson, Jessi Colter, and Tompall Glaser.
73. B) Ty Herndon—Herndon fronted the Tennessee River Boys, which changed its name to Diamond Rio after adding Roe and signing with Arista Records.
74. D) Hank Williams
75. D) Hank Williams Jr.
76. C) David Allan Coe
77. B) Sam Bush
78. B) Duane Eddy
79. B) Dean Dillon
80. B) Jerry Douglas
81. C) Whitey Ford (The Duke of Paducah)
82. B) *Blood on the Tracks*
83. B) BeauSoleil
84. A) Eddy Arnold—Arnold's 28 chart-topping singles have spent a cumulative total of 145 weeks—or just 11 weeks shy of three years—at #1.
85. B) Waylon Jennings
86. D) Donnie Young
87. C) Neal McCoy
88. B) Carl Smith
89. A) *The Apostle*
90. B) Earl Thomas Conley
91. B) *The Electric Horseman*
92. C) Vince Gill
93. D) War Memorial Auditorium—All four buildings served as home to the Opry, but the show broadcast from War Memorial from July 1939 until it moved to the Ryman in June 1943.
94. D) Sons of the Desert
95. D) Mark Chesnutt

96. D) Ray Charles—Charles has eight Top Forty country hits, most of them duets—none of them from his seminal *Modern Sounds in Country & Western* album.
97. B) Buddy Emmons
98. A) Exile
99. C) Donna Fargo
100. C) Multiple sclerosis (MS)
101. B) Freddy Fender
102. C) A.C. "Eck" Robertson
103. A) Jo Dee Messina
104. C) Kenny Rogers
105. A) Ronnie Milsap
106. B) The Judds
107. B) Merle Haggard
108. D) Tennessee Ernie Ford
109. B) Forester Sisters—June's first name is actually Karen—just in case you wondered where the "K" sound went.
110. D) George Morgan
111. B) Nine Inch Nails
112. C) 1,352
113. C) Ken Nelson
114. B) 1992
115. A) Merle Haggard
116. D) *Tremors*
117. D) *WLS Barn Dance*, Chicago—Known most famously as the *National Barn Dance*, the *WLS Barn Dance* first broadcast April 19, 1924. The show that would become the Grand Ole Opry, the *WSM Barn Dance*, didn't air until November 1925, though it would long outlive the WLS show.
118. D) Tuberculosis
119. B) Garth Brooks's *Ropin' the Wind*—*Ropin' the Wind* debuted atop the chart September 28, 1991.
120. C) Noel
121. C) Spade Cooley

— TRIVIA QUIZ ANSWERS —

122. A) Curly Chalker—Harold Lee "Curly" Chalker, who would go on to play on Marie Osmond's "Paper Roses," Simon & Garfunkel's "The Boxer," and many other sessions, made his recording debut on this session.
123. B) Richard Petty
124. B) Dire Straits
125. B) Louise Mandrell—A younger sister of Barbara Mandrell, Louise had 16 Top Forty hits between 1979 and 1987, including "I Wanna Say Yes" and "I'm Not Through Loving You Yet."
126. C) Patty Loveless—The couple married February 6, 1989.
127. C) Jim Seales
128. B) $48
129. C) Pure Prairie League—Pure Prairie League's "Let Me Love You Tonight," with Vince Gill on lead vocals, hit the pop Top Ten in 1980.
130. A) Dale Earnhardt
131. C) Grape
132. C) Marty Robbins
133. C) Oak Ridge Boys
134. D) Dan Seals
135. A) Deana Carter
136. B) Vince Gill
137. C) Anne Murray
138. C) Grinder's Switch
139. D) Trigger
140. D) Bryan White—White's voice was mixed out of some subsequent versions of "From This Moment On."
141. B) *Annie Get Your Gun*
142. B) Reba McEntire
143. B) Larry Gatlin & the Gatlin Brothers
144. C) England Dan & John Ford Coley
145. A) Bryan Adams—Adams wrote the song with Robert John "Mutt" Lange.
146. A) Clint Black—Clint Black on March 25, 1989, with "Better Man."
147. C) Kenny Rogers—Five times. Randy Travis is second with four nominations.
148. B) $1.98

149. A) Dixie Chicks
150. A) Eddy Arnold
151. B) George Jones
152. A) Johnny Cash
153. B) Webb Pierce
154. D) 6—George Morgan had the biggest hit with the song, but Elton Britt, Red Foley, Cowboy Copas, Eddie Kirk, and Bud Hobbs also charted.
155. C) Waylon Jennings
156. A) Anaheim Angels
157. D) Freddy Weller
158. A) Flatt & Scruggs—Flatt & Scruggs recorded "The Ballad of Jed Clampett."
159. A) 22
160. A) 1962
161. B) Bob Luman
162. A) Hawkshaw Hawkins
163. B) An Internet chain letter
164. C) Alto saxophone
165. A) Bill Anderson
166. C) Alan Jackson
167. B) Plane crash—Reeves died in a plane crash on July 31, 1965.
168. A) Tom T. Hall
169. C) David Houston
170. B) Harlan Howard
171. A) $35,000
172. B) Millie Kirkham—Kirkham was one of Nashville's top session singers. Her voice also appears on Ferlin Husky's "Gone" and several Elvis Presley recordings.
173. C) Connie Smith
174. B) Brothers-in-law—Jack Anglin married Johnnie Wright's sister Louise.
175. C) Curtis Stone—Stone is the son of Hall of Famer Cliffie Stone.
176. B) Peter Jennings

177. C) Billy Joe Shaver
178. C) Dolly Parton
179. D) West of Austin
180. C) Hank Snow
181. C) Ray Price
182. D) Willie Nelson
183. D) RCA
184. D) Don Williams
185. D) Hank Williams Jr.
186. D) Hank Williams
187. A) Al Dexter
188. D) Allen Reynolds
189. D) Grady Martin
190. A) Eddie Cochran
191. B) Harlan Howard
192. D) Ray Price
193. B) Chris LeDoux
194. C) Jerry Reed
195. C) Gary Morris
196. B) Ferlin Husky
197. A) Rex Allen
198. A) Bud Isaacs
199. A) Cincinnati Bengals
200. D) It was the date he made his only Grand Ole Opry appearance.
201. C) Gary Morris
202. A) Clifton Clowers
203. B) Chris LeDoux
204. C) Johnny
205. C) Johnny Cash
206. B) Kenny Price

207. C) Tracy Lawrence
208. B) A grand piano covered in 24-karat gold leaf
209. C) Kathy Mattea
210. B) Jim Reeves
211. A) Barbecue
212. B) KWKH
213. B) Buddy Harman
214. C) Larry Stewart
215. C) *Lonely Grill*
216. C) Pittsburgh
217. B) Hepatitis
218. B) Nova Scotia
219. B) Felina
220. B) K.T. Oslin
221. D) Prince Albert Smoking Tobacco
222. B) Ray Price
223. D) Faron Young
224. C) Merle Haggard
225. A) Anita Carter—Anita recorded the song, written by June Carter and Merle Kilgore, under the title "Love's Ring of Fire."
226. C) *The Midnight Jamboree*
227. C) Mindy McCready
228. B) McReynolds
229. A) *Same Train, a Different Time: Merle Haggard Sings the Great Songs of Jimmie Rodgers*—Haggard released the album in 1969.
230. B) Cousin
231. C) Nikki Nelson
232. B) Don Rich
233. C) Paul Overstreet—Overstreet was married to Parton's younger sister Frieda from May 1975 to November 1976.

234. C) Pamper Music
235. A) Homer & Jethro
236. A) Loretta Lynn
237. C) Presley's Jubilee
238. D) Republican Party
239. C) RCA Studio B
240. A) Garth Brooks
241. D) Hazel Smith
242. C) Ronnie Milsap
243. C) Roy Clark—Clark first subbed for Johnny Carson in 1963.
244. D) Gary Gatlin
245. C) Sonny James
246. B) Jordanaires—The quartet, which formed as a gospel group in Missouri, has sung behind Elvis Presley, Patsy Cline, and dozens of other acts.
247. C) Spade Cooley
248. B) Rubber Duck
249. B) Tennessee Ernie Ford
250. D) Faron Young
251. A) Samantha Bumgarner and Eva Davis
252. C) The Judds—The film also featured Naomi's classically restored 1957 Chevy.
253. B) *Big River*
254. D) Sweet potato
255. B) Jim & Jesse
256. A) *In Old Santa Fe*
257. C) The Young Sheriff—Faron's nickname was "The Young Sheriff," but Charley Pride was known to refer to him as "the little banty rooster."
258. C) Tim McGraw
259. C) Toby Keith
260. C) Tom T. Hall—The single, Hall's first for RCA, was called "May the Force Be with You Always," and it reached #13.

261. A) Chad Brock
262. C) True love
263. D) Charlene Tilton
264. B) Martina McBride
265. C) Lorrie Morgan
266. B) New Jersey—Black was born in Long Branch, New Jersey, February 4, 1962.
267. C) Webb Pierce
268. B) George Jones
269. D) Jesse Taylor—The song was Dallas Frazier's "The Baptism of Jesse Taylor."
270. A) Jack Greene
271. D) Jerry Reed
272. A) Willie Nelson & Leon Russell, *One for the Road*—Nelson's album with Russell came out in 1979.
273. D) A palmetto tree and a crescent moon—It's the state emblem of South Carolina, Tippin's home state.
274. D) 33
275. C) 45—Oslin first hit with "Wall of Tears" in February 1987. The next year, she won the Country Music Association's Female Vocalist of the Year award.
276. C) 41
277. B) "The Last Dance"
278. B) April 1, 1967
279. B) Alcohol poisoning—Whitley died May 9, 1989.
280. D) Ernest Tubb
281. B) Charlotte Johnson
282. D) Jimmy Dean
283. A) 1969
284. D) WSM
285. A) Ted Daffan
286. D) Aaron Tippin
287. C) March 6, 1983—It was then known as CMTV.
288. C) *Five Easy Pieces*
289. C) Fiddle

290. B) Alan Jackson
291. B) Crystal Gayle
292. A) Clint Black
293. B) Bellamy Brothers
294. D) Steve Wariner
295. C) Billy Sherrill
296. B) Bobbie Ann Mason
297. A) All-4-One
298. A) Steve Buckingham
299. A) *Bob Roberts*
300. D) Southern Pacific—Drummer Keith Knudsen and guitarist John McFee had played with the Doobies; Stu Cook was CCR's bassist.
301. C) Ricky Skaggs
302. B) Diamond Rio
303. B) Toby Keith
304. B) Richie McDonald—McDonald was born February 6, 1962. Rainwater was born January 24, 1963; Britt on June 15, 1966; and Sams on August 3, 1966.
305. D) Trisha Yearwood
306. C) Charley Pride
307. B) David Cobb—Cobb, a WSM announcer, used the phrase on Red Foley's NBC radio show in 1950.
308. A) Brooks & Dunn—As of mid-2003, Brooks & Dunn had topped the *Billboard* country singles chart 17 times.
309. D) Bob Wills
310. B) *Esquire*
311. B) Drums
312. A) Dusty Chandler
313. D) Gene Watson
314. D) Phil Vassar
315. C) Randy Travis
316. D) Travis Tritt
317. C) Collin Raye

318. C) Joe Diffie
319. D) Bob Seger
320. A) Conway Twitty—Twitty died June 5, 1993.
321. A) Doug Stone
322. A) Terri Clark
323. D) George Jones
324. D) Mandolin
325. B) Fifty cents
326. D) Don Williams
327. C) Tex Ritter
328. B) Gene Autry—Autry's chart span is 55 years, 11 months, one week.
329. C) Fred Rose—Rose, a songwriter, co-founded Nashville's first country music publishing house, Acuff-Rose Publications, with Roy Acuff in 1942.
330. C) Buck Owens
331. A) Minnie Pearl
332. C) Kenny Rogers, *Greatest Hits*—Rogers's *Greatest Hits* spent two weeks on top of the chart in December 1980.
333. C) Delia "Mom" Upchurch
334. A) Red Foley—*Ozark Jubilee*, also known as *Country Music Jubilee* and *Jubilee U.S.A.*, aired from 1955 to 1961.
335. D) *Urban Cowboy*
336. B) Huey Lewis
337. B) In a buffalo herd
338. C) *Ten Feet Tall and Bulletproof*
339. D) Porter Wagoner
340. A) Billy Joe Royal
341. A) Roy Acuff
342. C) Shania Twain
343. D) Rick Treviño
344. B) John Denver—Both "Thank God I'm a Country Boy" and "I'm Sorry" hit #1 on both charts in 1975.

345. A) Johnny Bush
346. B) Johnny Rodriguez
347. B) Joy Lynn White
348. C) *Love Me Tender*
349. C) Kenny Rogers
350. A) Quaker State Oil Convention
351. C) Dottie West
352. D) Clay Walker
353. B) Mark Miller
354. D) Trisha Yearwood
355. B) Marty Roe
356. C) Hargus "Pig" Robbins
357. D) Townes Van Zandt
358. B) Mom's
359. B) Moon Mullican
360. B) Owen Bradley
361. C) Bruce Robison
362. D) *Robin Hood*
363. D) Dwight Yoakam—Yoakam played an abusive boyfriend named Doyle Hargraves.
364. C) Floyd Tillman
365. A) George Jones—But Red Sovine & Webb Pierce's version went to #1 in 1956; Jones's 1955 version peaked at #4.
366. D) The Tractors
367. D) Frank Sinatra—After Presley's death, Sinatra said: "There have been many accolades uttered about Elvis's talent and performances through the years, all of which I agree with wholeheartedly. I shall miss him dearly as a friend. He was a warm, considerate, and generous man."
368. B) Richard Sterban
369. C) Marty Stuart
370. D) John Travolta
371. A) Raul Malo

372. C) Hargus "Pig" Robbins
373. C) Billy Swan
374. B) Shel Silverstein
375. C) Connie Smith
376. B) Sonny Curtis—Curtis also backed Buddy Holly on his first commercial recordings.
377. C) Hayden Nicholas
378. C) Patty Loveless
379. C) Webb Pierce—Pierce eventually switched out the silver dollars for alloy coins.
380. D) Mel Tillis
381. D) Marty Robbins
382. C) Jim Reeves
383. D) Trigger—It's a Martin N-20 nylon-string acoustic guitar. Nelson bought it from Nashville steel-guitar great Shot Jackson for $750.
384. D) Nitty Gritty Dirt Band
385. C) *The Smothers Brothers Comedy Hour*
386. C) Sweethearts of the Rodeo
387. D) *The Waltons*
388. C) Marty Robbins
389. C) Don Schlitz & Paul Overstreet
390. D) Stringbean (Dave Akeman)
391. B) Waylon Jennings
392. D) T. Texas Tyler
393. B) We Shield Millions—"We Shield Millions" was the slogan of the station's original owners, the National Life and Accident Insurance Company.
394. A) Billy Gilman—Gilman's 1988 hit "One Voice" entered the *Billboard* chart three days after his 12th birthday.
395. A) *Strait Country*
396. B) Dann Huff
397. C) Spontaneous Combustion
398. D) Faron Young

399. D) Brenda Lee—Brenda Lee is four feet, nine inches tall—two inches shorter than Dickens and ten inches shorter than Pee Wee King.

400. C) Marc Cohn—Cohn's "Walking in Memphis" was a Top Twenty pop hit in 1991 and led to his winning a Best New Artist Grammy.

401. C) Steven Seagal

402. D) Kim Williams—Williams's hits include "If the Devil Danced in Empty Pockets," "The Heart Is a Lonely Hunter," and several Brooks hits, including "Papa Loved Mama" and "Ain't Goin' Down ('t il the Sun Comes Up)."

403. B) Julie

404. D) *The Simpsons*

405. D) Ralph Stanley

406. D) Spider monkey

407. A) Deerhurst Resort

408. B) Alan Jackson

409. C) J.D. Sumner

410. C) Scott Hendricks

411. B) John Conlee

412. D) Leon Russell

413. B) The Bowery

414. B) Bennett Vartanian

415. D) Doralee Rhodes

416. C) *Now That I've Found You: A Collection*, Alison Krauss—After the nominations were announced, the CMA realized that Krauss's album consisted primarily of previously released material, thereby making it ineligible for the award.

417. C) Loretta Haggers—Under the billing "Mary Kay Place as Loretta Haggers," she actually had a #3 single with "Baby Boy" in 1976.

418. B) Englebert Humperdinck—Humperdinck, who hit the country Top 40 in 1977 with "After the Lovin'," was born Arnold George Dorsey in Madras, India.

419. A) *Eyes That See in the Dark*—The album includes Rogers's smash duet with Dolly Parton, "Islands in the Stream."

— TRIVIA QUIZ ANSWERS —

420. A) Barbara Mandrell—The September 11, 1984, wreck left Mandrell with several broken bones and a concussion.

421. B) Willie Nelson—As of mid-2003, Nelson had had charting hits with 21 different artists—22 if you count his 1984 "Wabash Cannonball" with Hank Wilson, a pseudonym for Leon Russell ("Heartbreak Hotel," 1979).

422. D) *Johnnie High's Country Music Revue*, Fort Worth

423. D) Ernest Tubb—Tubb's hits included the 1964 record "Thanks a Lot."

424. B) 1980

425. C) 1989

426. B) "How-dee!"

427. D) A blind piano tuner

428. D) A leprechaun—The tattoo symbolizes McGraw's "good luck."

429. C) Al Dexter—The singles were "Pistol Packin' Mama," "Rosalita," "So Long Pal," "Too Late to Worry," and "I'm Losing My Mind over You."

430. C) Alan Jackson—Jackson debuted on the show—and Brooks joined it—October 6, 1990.

431. C) Allen Reynolds—Don Was produced the *Chris Gaines* project.

432. A) Garth Brooks—*Country Weekly* launched April 12, 1994, with Garth Brooks on its cover. Randy Travis and Mary Chapin Carpenter had inset photos, and a Faith Hill feature was also touted.

433. C) Bob Moore

434. A) Johnny Cash

435. D) Little Feat

436. A) Bashful Brother Oswald—Oswald, also known as Beecher "Pete" Kirby, first appeared on the Grand Ole Opry January 7, 1939. He continued playing the Opry following Acuff's death and passed away in October 2002.

437. B) George D. Hay

438. A) Lynn Anderson

439. B) Jimmy Colvard

440. D) Little David Wilkins—Wilkins, who actually weighed more than 200 pounds, had a handful of hits during the 1970s, most notably 1975's "One Monkey Don't Stop No Show." He never did record "T-R-O-U-B-L-E," though.

441. A) Eddy Arnold
442. A) *Creeps Like Me*
443. A) Baillie & the Boys—Alan LeBoeuf, a member of the group until 1989, played McCartney.
444. B) Lee Greenwood—When asked to be a part of the new band, Greenwood turned down the offer because he had a guaranteed income in Las Vegas.
445. D) Sheb Wooley
446. D) Hurricane Mills
447. D) Okinawa, Japan—Tillis was stationed in Okinawa while he was in the air force.
448. C) *Ironside*
449. B) Terri Clark
450. A) Sherrié Austin
451. D) Becky Thatcher
452. D) Tammy Wynette
453. D) Billy Joe Shaver
454. A) Faith Hill
455. C) J.P. Pennington—Additionally, Country Music Hall of Famer Red Foley was Pennington's uncle.
456. C) Joe Stampley—As Traywick, Travis released two Stampley-produced singles, "Dreams" and "She's My Woman," which reached #91 on the *Billboard* country singles chart.
457. C) John Michael Montgomery—Eddie Montgomery is John Michael's older brother.
458. C) John Rich—The following year, the group released its *Lonely Grill* album, which included such hits as "Amazed," "Smile," and "What About Now." Rich's debut solo single, "I Pray for You," peaked at #53.
459. C) Canyon
460. D) Wal-Mart
461. A) Bristol—The city straddled the Tennessee-Virginia border.
462. D) The Skyline
463. A) Emmylou Harris
464. C) Lyle Lovett
465. C) *Mad*
466. C) Nitty Gritty Dirt Band
467. A) Charlie Daniels

468. B) Chely Wright
469. D) The Outlaws
470. B) Louisville, Kentucky
471. D) Blaine Sprouse
472. D) Statler Brothers
473. B) *Ocean Front Property*, George Strait
474. C) Pitcher
475. B) *The Girl Can't Help It*
476. A) American civilization
477. C) Quacker
478. D) Sawyer Brown's Mark Miller—Miller played guard for the Ft. Wayne Fury of the minor-league Continental Basketball Association in 1997 and 1998.
479. C) Rob Reiner
480. B) Nashville Palace
481. D) Steve Wariner
482. B) Anne Murray
483. D) Sandi Spika—Spika began designing dresses for McEntire in 1986.
484. D) Thumper Jones
485. C) Southern Doughnuts
486. D) Sawyer Brown
487. B) *College of Musical Knowledge*
488. A) *Bye Bye Birdie*
489. B) The Judds
490. A) Forester Sisters
491. B) The Highwaymen
492. A) Ken Curtis
493. B) Mac Davis
494. B) Brother Phelps
495. C) Olivia Newton-John
496. B) John Denver
497. A) Patsy Cline

498. C) Van Stephenson
499. B) Ferlin Husky
500. C) Roger Miller
501. B) Lacy J. Dalton
502. A) John Berry
503. A) Crystal Gayle—Crystal's given name is Brenda Gail Webb. Her sister Loretta Lynn got the idea for her stage name when she passed a Krystal.
504. A) Byrds
505. C) From kicking his mother while he was in the womb—Kix's given name is Leon Eric Brooks.
506. C) Dolly Parton—Dolly Parton has 24 chart-topping *Billboard* singles, followed by McEntire's 21, Wynette's 20, and Gayle's 19.
507. D) $16.7 million
508. D) Hank Williams Jr.—He won his Emmy in 1990 for his promotional spots for *Monday Night Football*.
509. B) Collin Wray—As a member of the Wray Brothers Band and, later, the Wrays, Collin billed himself as Bubba Wray.
510. B) Ben Colder
511. C) Robert John "Mutt" Lange—Lange began producing Twain's albums beginning with her second, *The Woman in Me*.
512. C) Luke the Drifter Jr.
513. D) George Morgan
514. B) Eagle
515. D) Hank Thompson
516. D) Pam Tillis
517. A) Johnny Horton
518. C) Marty Robbins
519. A) Bill Anderson
520. A) New Grass Revival
521. B) Gene Autry
522. A) Razzy Bailey
523. B) T. Graham Brown
524. C) Terri Gibbs

525. A) Terry Bradshaw
526. B) Mark Chesnutt
527. C) Billy Joel
528. B) Jimmie Davis
529. C) George Jones & Tammy Wynette
530. C) Norma Jean
531. A) Rodney Crowell
532. B) Ernest Tubb
533. A) The 1903 wreck of Southern Railways Engine 1102 near Danville, Virginia
534. B) 229 Jackson Street
535. A) Cop
536. B) Gospel—Pride won 1971 Grammys for Best Sacred Performance (*Did You Think to Pray?*) and Best Gospel Performance (Other Than Soul Gospel) ("Let Me Live"). He won his first country Grammy the following year.
537. C) Garth Brooks—Brooks has placed 12 different Christmas singles on the charts, most notably "Belleau Wood," which peaked at #41 in 1999.
538. A) Alabama—Between 1980 and 1987, Alabama had 21 consecutive #1 singles.
539. C) *Hidden Guns*—Young played a deputy in the film.
540. D) February 16, 1969
541. D) *True Grit*
542. B) Coffee & bourbon
543. B) Boudleaux Bryant
544. D) The restaurant was still open.
545. B) *The Milagro Beanfield War*
546. D) Billy Parker—Between 1976 and 1989, Parker—a former member of Ernest Tubb's band—charted 22 times. His best showing came in 1982 with "(Who's Gonna Sing) the Last Country Song." It peaked at #41.
547. B) Luttrell
548. C) Freddie Hart
549. D) "The Snakes Crawl at Night"—Pride's first five singles also were credited to Country Charley Pride.

COUNTRY
Q&A

1. **Who were the first singers inducted into the Country Music Hall of Fame?**

2. Who is the only performer inducted into the Country Music Hall of Fame twice?

3. **Match the artists to the labels that released some of their hits:**

1. Alabama	A) Barnaby
2. Johnny Cash	B) Cadence
3. Holly Dunn	C) Challenge
4. Everly Brothers	D) Dot
5. Donna Fargo	E) Little Darlin'
6. Mickey Gilley	F) MDJ
7. The Kendalls	G) MTM
8. Loretta Lynn	H) Ovation
9. Johnny Paycheck	I) Plantation
10. Jeannie C. Riley	J) Playboy
11. Ray Stevens	K) Sun
12. Wynn Stewart	L) Zero

4. What song had the longest title ever to hit *Billboard*'s country Top Forty?

5. **Match the artists to the labels that released some of their hits:**

1. Lynn Anderson	A) 4 Star
2. Ernest Ashworth	B) Abbott
3. Johnny Bush	C) Chart
4. Roy Clark	D) Compleat
5. Vern Gosdin	E) Dot
6. Mark McGuinn	F) Hickory
7. Roger Miller	G) Imperial
8. Jim Reeves	H) Kapp
9. Sammi Smith	I) Mega
10. Mel Tillis	J) Smash
11. "T" Texas Tyler	K) Stop
12. Slim Whitman	L) VFR

6. What were the two men who killed Grand Ole Opry star Stringbean and his wife in 1973 looking for?

Answers begin on page 99.

7. **What's the only Top Forty country single with a title that begins with the letter "X"?**

8. How tall is Little Jimmy Dickens?

9. **Match the acts with their sole Top Forty country hit:**

   1. Kay Adams   A) "Bad News"
   2. Billy Hill   B) "The Battle of New Orleans"
   3. Boxcar Willie   C) "Callin' Baton Rouge"
   4. Jimmie Driftwood   D) "Deck of Cards"
   5. Harlan Howard   E) "Fairytale"
   6. Lonesome Strangers   F) "Goodbye Lonesome, Hello Baby Doll"
   7. Wink Martindale   G) "Little Pink Mack"
   8. New Grass Revival   H) "Too Much Month at the End of the Money"
   9. Perfect Stranger   I) "You Have the Right to Remain Silent"
   10. Pointer Sisters   J) "Sunday Morning Christian"

10. What do Mickey Gilley, Jerry Lee Lewis, and evangelist Jimmy Swaggart have in common?

11. **What country legend wore this suit, fashioned by California tailor Nudie?**

12. What was the original name of Roy Acuff's Smoky Mountain Boys?

13. **Name five artists who had a hit with "The Tip of My Fingers."**

14. Where did Billy "Crash" Craddock get his nickname?

15. **What piano-playing technique did Floyd Cramer popularize on records like Hank Locklin's "Please Help Me, I'm Falling" and his own "Last Date."**

16. How were Skeeter Davis and Betty Jack Davis—the Davis Sisters—related?

(see question #11)

Answers begin on page 99.

17. How did Conway Twitty get his name?

18. What other people died in the March 5, 1963, plane crash that killed Patsy Cline?

(see question #21)

19. Who was banjo player and former New Grass Revival member Béla Fleck named after?

20. What two country classics did Don Gibson write on the same day?

21. What Country Music Hall of Famer would have crooned his elegant ballads in this tuxedo jacket?

22. Which member of Brooks & Dunn had more singles chart success as a solo act?

23. How did the dobro get its name?

24. Where did the Bellamy Brothers' David Bellamy get the inspiration for "If I Said You Had a Beautiful Body Would You Hold It against Me"?

25. Each of the following acts had only one record reach the *Billboard* country chart, but it was a Top Ten hit. Match the act with the single:

1. Jimmy Boyd	A) "Too Young to Tango"
2. Owen Bradley Quintet	B) "Blues Stay Away from Me"
3. Del Wood	C) "Cry of the Dying Duck in a Thunder-Storm"
4. Ralph Emery	D) "Down Yonder"
5. Bill Justis & His Orchestra	E) "Giddyup Go—Answer"
6. Vaughn Monroe	F) "Hello Fool"
7. Minnie Pearl	G) "Hot Rod Race"
8. Cactus Pryor & His Pricklypears	H) "I Saw Mommy Kissing Santa Claus"
9. Arkie Shibley & His Mountain Dew Boys	I) "Raunchy"
10. Sunshine Ruby	J) "Riders in the Sky (a Cowboy Legend)"

26. Who is Deana Carter's father?

*Answers begin on page 99.

27. What two songs did the Byrds sing when they appeared on the Grand Ole Opry March 15, 1968?

28. Who comprised the country supergroup the Highwaymen?

29. **Where did Jessi Colter get her name?**

30. How did Floyd Cramer make the pickaxe sounds on Jimmy Dean's 1961 smash "Big Bad John"?

31. **Match the bluegrass act with its backing band:**

    1. Flatt & Scruggs
    2. Lester Flatt
    3. Jim & Jesse
    4. Jimmy Martin
    5. Bill Monroe
    6. Charlie Monroe
    7. Ricky Skaggs

    A) Blue Grass Boys
    B) Foggy Mountain Boys
    C) Kentucky Partners
    D) Kentucky Thunder
    E) Nashville Grass
    F) Sunny Mountain Boys
    G) Virginia Boys

32. Which Grand Ole Opry star had the same initials as the call letters of the station on which the show is broadcast?

33. **Match the artist with her nickname:**

    1. Dale Evans
    2. Linda Hargrove
    3. Brenda Lee
    4. Loretta Lynn
    5. Barbara Mandrell
    6. Jeannie Seely
    7. Connie Smith
    8. Kitty Wells
    9. Del Wood
    10. Tammy Wynette

    A) Blue Jean Country Queen
    B) Coal Miner's Daughter
    C) First Lady of Country Music
    D) Little Miss Dynamite
    E) Miss Country Soul
    F) Princess of the Steel
    G) Queen of Country Music
    H) Queen of the Ivories
    I) Queen of the West
    J) Sweetheart of the Grand Ole Opry

34. What words encircle the rotunda of the Country Music Hall of Fame?

*Answers begin on page 99.

35. Which two of her songs has Mary Chapin Carpenter turned into children's books?

36. Which of Loretta Lynn's siblings had charting country hits?

Tammy Wynette

37. **Which country artists participated in the 1985 "We Are the World" recording session?**

38. What did Hillary Rodham Clinton say on *60 Minutes* in 1992 that incensed Tammy Wynette?

39. **Who were the members of the Browns?**

40. What was the name of Glen Campbell's variety show for CBS-TV, and when did it air?

41. **Who were the original three members of Dave & Sugar?**

42. What's the connection between Dolly Parton and *Buffy the Vampire Slayer*?

43. **Who were the original members of the Carter Family?**

44. Who performed at the first Farm Aid?

45. **Match the act to the song with which it had a hit:**

1. John Anderson	A) "Don't Cheat in Our Hometown"
2. Moe Bandy	B) "I Cheated on a Good Woman's Love"
3. Brooks & Dunn	C) "If I Had a Cheating Heart"
4. Billy "Crash" Craddock	D) "It's a Cheatin' Situation"
5. The Kendalls	E) "Last Cheater's Waltz"
6. Charly McClain	F) "She Just Started Liking Cheatin' Songs"
7. T.G. Sheppard	G) "She's Not the Cheatin' Kind"
8. Ricky Skaggs	H) "Teach Me to Cheat"
9. Mel Street	I) "Who's Cheatin' Who"
10. Hank Williams	J) "Your Cheatin' Heart"

Answers begin on page 99.

46. How many of the Statler Brothers are brothers?

47. **Match the singer with her given name:**

1. Patsy Cline	A) Jean Bowman
2. Jessi Colter	B) Myrna Joy Brooks
3. Lacy J. Dalton	C) Jill Byrem
4. Skeeter Davis	D) Christina Claire Ciminella
5. Crystal Gayle	E) Sarah Ophelia Colley
6. Faith Hill	F) Muriel Ellen Deason
7. Jan Howard	G) Eileen Edwards
8. Naomi Judd	H) Virginia Patterson Hensley
9. Wynonna Judd	I) Mirriam Johnson
10. Jeannie Kendall	J) Lula Grace Johnson
11. Brenda Lee	K) Diana Ellen Judd
12. Jody Miller	L) Jeannie Kuykendall
13. Minnie Pearl	M) Dorothy Marie Marsh
14. Jeanne Pruett	N) Constance June Meador
15. Jeannie C. Riley	O) Mary Frances Penick
16. Connie Smith	P) Audrey Faith Perry
17. Kitty Wells	Q) Virginia Wynette Pugh
18. Shania Twain	R) Jeanne Carolyn Stephenson
19. Dottie West	S) Brenda Mae Tarpley
20. Tammy Wynette	T) Brenda Gaylor Webb

48. Shania Twain and LeAnn Rimes share a birthday. What is it?

49. **What was Johnny Cash's first single release for Sun Records?**

50. Who was the first country singer to host *Saturday Night Live*?

51. **Patsy Cline and Harlan Howard—who wrote several songs Cline recorded, including "I Fall to Pieces"—shared a birthday. What is it?**

52. Where did the group BR5-49 gets its name?

Answers begin on page 99.

53. Match the country act with the backing band:

1. Gary Allan	A) 911
2. Garth Brooks	B) Ace in the Hole Band
3. Tracy Byrd	C) Babylonian Cowboys
4. Kenny Chesney	D) Dancehall Doctors
5. Steve Earle	E) Dukes
6. Alan Jackson	F) Easy Money
7. Toby Keith	G) Fabulous Falls
8. Tracy Lawrence	H) His Large Band
9. Lyle Lovett	I) Honky Tonk Wranglers
10. Tim McGraw	J) Little Elvis
11. Lorrie Morgan	K) Mr. Nasty
12. Rascal Flatts	L) Mystic Biscuits
13. George Strait	M) No Mercy
14. Marty Stuart	N) Nokintobob
15. Pam Tillis	O) Only Way to Fly
16. Aaron Tippin	P) Rock & Roll Cowboys
17. Shania Twain	Q) Stemwinders
18. Mark Wills	R) Stillwater
19. Lee Ann Womack	S) Strayhorns
20. Dwight Yoakam	Y) TBA

54. Who were the first and last artists to record live albums at the Houston Astrodome?

55. Match the session musician with his instrument:

1. Eddie Bayers	A) Acoustic guitar
2. Paul Franklin	B) Bass
3. Rob Hajacos	C) Dobro
4. Rob Ickes	D) Drums
5. Brent Mason	E) Electric guitar
6. Terry McMillan	F) Fiddle
7. Matt Rollings	G) Harmonica
8. Bryan Sutton	H) Piano
9. Glenn Worf	I) Steel guitar

Answers begin on page 99.

56. Who hosted *Hee Haw*?

57. Jo Dee Messina and Billy Ray Cyrus share a birthday. What is it?

58. What country singer was named after a Confederate general?

59. What beloved country comedienne wore this straw hat on stage?

60. Where did Hank Williams Jr. get the nickname "Bocephus"?

61. Who won *Nashville Star*, USA Network's talent-search show, in 2003?

62. What's the connection between C.W. McCall and Mannheim Steamroller?

(see question #59)

63. What country singers have appeared as guest voices on *The Simpsons*?

64. Match these songs recorded by Johnny Cash with the rock or pop act that previously had recorded them:

1. "Bird on a Wire"	A) Leonard Cohen
2. "Don't Think Twice It's Alright"	B) Danzig
3. "I Hung My Head"	C) Depeche Mode
4. "I Won't Back Down"	D) Neil Diamond
5. "Johnny 99"	E) Bob Dylan
6. "Personal Jesus"	F) Nick Lowe
7. "Rusty Cage"	G) Tom Petty
8. "Solitary Man"	H) Soundgarden
9. "The Beast in Me"	I) Bruce Springsteen
10. "Thirteen"	J) Sting

65. Who was Rufus "Tee Tot" Payne, and why is he important to country music?

Answers begin on page 99.

66. **What's the inscription on Patsy Cline's gravestone?**

67. What Country Music Hall of Fame songwriting team wrote such hits as the Everly Brothers' "Bye Bye Love," Little Jimmy Dickens's "Country Boy," and the Osborne Brothers' "Rocky Top"?

(see question #69)

68. **What's the connection between Clint Black's wife, Lisa Hartman Black, and the 1960s television sitcom *Bewitched*?**

69. What country-rocker wore this Nudie-designed jacket with symbols that blended country roots with a rock & roll attitude?

70. **Name Emmylou Harris's three backing bands.**

71. What 1980s country hit was inspired by the pop group Culture Club and its cross-dressing lead singer, Boy George?

72. **What kind of car was George Jones driving when he had his near-fatal 1999 wreck?**

73. To what singer did Merle Haggard pay tribute with his 1981 hit "Leonard"?

74. **Match these songs recorded by Willie Nelson with the rock or pop act that previously had recorded them:**

1. "Don't Give Up"	A) Gregg Allman
2. "Fire and Rain"	B) Everly Brothers
3. "Graceland"	C) Peter Gabriel
4. "Heart of Gold"	D) Cyndi Lauper
5. "Let It Be Me"	E) Platters
6. "Midnight Rider"	F) Paul Simon
7. "Time after Time"	G) James Taylor
8. "Twilight Time"	H) Neil Young

*Answers begin on page 99.

75. What singer retired from performing shortly after hitting #1 with her debut single, "What I Really Meant to Say," in 2001?

76. Match these songs recorded by Dolly Parton with the rock or pop act that previously had recorded them:

1. "Downtown"		A) Black
2. "Just When I Needed You Most"		B) Petula Clark
3. "Peace Train"		C) Collective Soul
4. "Save the Last Dance for Me"		D) Drifters
5. "Shine"		E) Billy Joel
6. "Stairway to Heaven"		F) Katrina & the Waves
7. "Time for Me to Fly"		G) Led Zeppelin
8. "Train, Train"		H) REO Speedwagon
9. "Travelin' Prayer"		I) Cat Stevens
10. "Walking on Sunshine"		J) Randy Vanwarmer

77. In 1965, Johnny Cash took out a full-page ad in *Billboard* chastising radio programmers who wouldn't play his single "The Ballad of Ira Hayes," about the Pima Indian and U.S. Marine who helped raise the American flag at Iwo Jima but later died from alcoholism and exposure at age 33. What did it say?

78. Match the country radio show with the station that broadcast it:

1. *Big D Jamboree*		A) KRLD, Dallas, Texas
2. *Jamboree, U.S.A.*		B) KWKH, Shreveport, Louisiana
3. *Louisiana Hayride*		C) KWTO, Springfield, Missouri
4. *Midday Merry-Go-Round*		D) WNOX, Knoxville, Tennessee
5. *Midwestern Hayride*		E) WLS, Chicago, Illinois
6. *National Barn Dance*		F) WRVA, Richmond, Virginia
7. *Old Dominion Barn Dance*		G) WWVA, Wheeling, West Virginia
8. *Ozark Jubilee*		H) WLW, Cincinnati, Ohio

79. Who was the first country artist to appear on the cover of *Rolling Stone*?

80. Who was the first country artist signed to Frank Sinatra's Reprise Records label?

*Answers begin on page 99.

George Jones

81. **Which country singers have performed the national anthem at the Super Bowl?**

82. Who was originally cast as Loretta Lynn's husband, Oliver "Mooney" Lynn, in the film *Coal Miner's Daughter* and later replaced by Tommy Lee Jones?

83. **What bluegrass-gospel act did Andy Griggs formerly back?**

84. Which member of Brooks & Dunn penned the #1 hits "I'm Only in It for the Love" for John Conlee and "Modern Day Romance" for the Nitty Gritty Dirt Band?

85. **Who told Roy Orbison, "You know, Roy, you need to do two things: change your name and lower your voice"?**

86. Who landed a helicopter on Johnny Cash's lawn in order to pitch him a demo tape of his songs?

87. **Match the name of the single with the person who sang it as a duet with George Jones.**

1. "Hallelujah, I Love You So"	A) Brenda Carter
2. "I've Got Five Dollars and It's Saturday Night"	B) Ray Charles
3. "Mabellene"	C) Merle Haggard
4. "Milwaukee, Here I Come"	D) Jeanette Hicks
5. "Waltz of the Angels"	E) Brenda Lee
6. "We Didn't See a Thing"	F) Melba Montgomery
7. "We Must Have Been Out of Our Minds"	G) Johnny Paycheck
8. "We're Gonna Hold On"	H) Gene Pitney
9. "Yearning"	I) Margie Singleton
10. "Yesterday's Wine"	J) Tammy Wynette

88. Where did Patsy Cline's last concert take place?

89. **Where did Johnny Cash propose to June Carter?**

Answers begin on page 99.

90. Match the session musician with his instrument:

1. Floyd Cramer	A) Acoustic bass
2. Pete Drake	B) Acoustic guitar
3. Ray Edenton	C) Drums
4. Hank Garland	D) Electric guitar
5. Buddy Harman	E) Fiddle
6. Tommy Jackson	F) Harmonica
7. Charlie McCoy	G) Piano
8. Bob Moore	H) Saxophone
9. Boots Randolph	I) Steel guitar

91. Match the session musician with his instrument:

1. Earle "Poole" Ball	A) Acoustic guitar
2. Mark Casstevens	B) Banjo
3. Johnny Gimble	C) Bass
4. Kenny Malone	D) Drums
5. J.D. Maness	E) Electric guitar
6. Joe Osbor	F) Fiddle
7. Bobby Thompson	G) Piano
8. Reggie Young	H) Steel guitar

92. Match the act to the song with which it had a hit:

1. Earl Thomas Conley	A) "Don't Come Home A' Drinkin'(with Lovin' on Your Mind)"
2. Charlie Daniels	B) "Drinkin' and Dreamin'"
3. Merle Haggard	C) "Drinkin' My Baby Goodbye"
4. Waylon Jennings	D) "Drinkin' My Baby (Off My Mind)"
5. George Jones	E) "Drinking Wine Spo-Dee O'Dee"
6. Jerry Lee Lewis	F) "I Think I'll Just Stay Here and Drink"
7. Loretta Lynn	G) "If Drinkin' Don't Kill Me (Her Memory Will)"
8. Eddie Rabbitt	H) "She's Actin' Single (I'm Drinkin' Doubles)"
9. Cal Smith	I) "The Lord Knows I'm Drinking"
10. Gary Stewart	J) "You Must Not Be Drinking Enough"

*Answers begin on page 99.

93. Match the singing cowboy/cowgirl with his/her horse:

1. Gene Autry	A) Apache
2. Bob Baker	B) Buttermilk
3. Dale Evans	C) Champion
4. Dick Foran	D) Lucky
5. Herb Jeffries	E) Smoke
6. Ken Maynard	F) Stardusk
7. Tex Ritter	G) Tarzan
8. Roy Rogers	H) Trigger
9. Jimmy Wakely	I) White Flash

94. Match the television show with its emcee/host:

1. *Country Playhouse*	A) Archie Campbell
2. *Hometown Jamboree*	B) Jimmy Dean
3. *Nashville Now*	C) "Toby" Dick Ellis
4. *Ozark Jubilee*	D) Ralph Emery
5. *Possum Holler Opry*	E) Red Foley
6. *Town & Country Jamboree*	F) Jay Stewart
7. *Town Hall Party*	G) Cliffie Stone

95. Match the act to the song with which it had a hit:

1. Bill Anderson	A) "Mama Don't Forget to Pray for Me"
2. Liz Anderson	B) "Mama Don't Get Dressed Up for Nothing"
3. Brooks & Dunn	C) "Mama He's Crazy"
4. John Conlee	D) "Mama Knows"
5. Diamond Rio	E) "Mama Sang a Song"
6. Forester Sisters	F) "Mama Spank"
7. Merle Haggard	G) "Mama Tried"
8. Waylon Jennings & Willie Nelson	H) "Mama's Never Seen Those Eyes"
9. The Judds	I) "Mama's Rockin' Chair"
10. Shenandoah	J) "Mammas Don't Let Your Babies Grow Up to Be Cowboys"

*Answers begin on page 99.

96. Match the artist with the name of his band:

1. Roy Acuff	A) Smoky Mountain Boys
2. Jim Ed Brown	B) Buckaroos
3. Johnny Cash	C) Waylors
4. Al Dexter	D) Cumberland Valley Boys
5. Red Foley	E) Drifting Cowboys
6. Ferlin Husky	F) Gems
7. Stonewall Jackson	G) Texas Troubadours
8. Waylon Jennings	H) His Troupers
9. Buck Owens	I) Hush Puppies
10. Webb Pierce	J) Wondering Boys
11. Ernest Tubb	K) Minutemen
12. Hank Williams	L) Tennessee Two

97. Match the artist with his nickname:

1. Eddy Arnold	A) Baron of Country Music
2. Dick Curless	B) Best Friend a Song Ever Had
3. Whitey Ford	C) Storyteller
4. Tom T. Hall	D) Dean of Nashville Songwriters
5. Harlan Howard	E) Tennessee Plowboy
6. George Jones	F) Duke of Paducah
7. Marty Robbins	G) Gentle Giant
8. Webb Pierce	H) Smilin' Star Duster
9. Charlie Rich	I) Wondering Boy
10. Conway Twitty	J) Mr. Tear Drop
11. Slim Whitman	K) Possum
12. Don Williams	L) Silver Fox

98. What Country Music Hall of Famer's mother made her this purple dress for one of her stage costumes?

99. What does the name "Shania" mean?

(see question #98)

Answers begin on page 99.

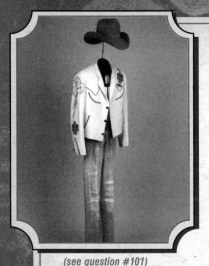

(see question #101)

100. Who is Tim McGraw's father?

101. What lanky singer squeezed himself into this western jacket and torn jeans?

102. Which *Dukes of Hazzard* star had the most Top Forty country hits?

103. After what actress was Loretta Lynn named?

104. For what two baseball greats was Roger Miller named?

105. When and where did Elvis Presley make his final concert appearance?

106. Match the singer with his given name:

1. Boxcar Willie	A) David Akeman	
2. Tommy Collins	B) William Neal Browder	
3. John Denver	C) John Henry Deutschendorf Jr.	
4. Dave Dudley	D) Jimmy Ellis	
5. Freddy Fender	E) William Fries	
6. Freddie Hart	F) Edward Garvin Futch	
7. Sonny James	G) Jerry Hubbard	
8. Cledus T. Judd	H) Baldemar G. Huerta	
9. Pee Wee King	I) Harold Lloyd Jenkins	
10. Dickey Lee	J) Julius Frank Kuczynski	
11. C.W. McCall	K) Royden Dickey Lipscombe	
12. Orion	L) James Hugh Loden	
13. Johnny Paycheck	M) Donald Eugene Lytle	
14. Eddy Raven	N) Lecil Travis Martin	
15. Jerry Reed	O) David Perduska	
16. Roy Rogers	P) Barry Poole	
17. T. G. Sheppard	Q) Frederick Segrest	
18. Stringbean	R) Leonard Raymond Sipes	
19. Randy Travis	S) Leonard Slye	
20. Conway Twitty	T) Randy Bruce Traywick	

*Answers begin on page 99.

1. Hank Williams and Jimmie Rodgers, in 1961.
2. Roy Rogers—first as a member of the Original Sons of the Pioneers in 1980, then as a solo act in 1988.
3. 1-F; 2-K; 3-G; 4-B; 5-D; 6-J; 7-H; 8-L; 9-E; 10-I; 11-A; 12-C
4. Nat Stuckey's 1970 single "She Wakes Me with a Kiss Every Morning (and She Loves Me to Sleep Every Night)"—at 78 characters.
5. 1-C; 2-F; 3-K; 4-E; 5-D; 6-L; 7-J; 8-B; 9-I; 10-H; 11-A; 12-G
6. John and Doug Brown were looking for a stash of money the Grand Ole Opry star supposedly had hidden in his house. Years later, the money was found, rotted and unusable, in the walls of Stringbean's house.
7. Trisha Yearwood's "XXX's and OOO's (An American Girl)"—which reached #1 in 1994.
8. 4 feet, 11 inches.
9. 1-G; 2-H; 3-A; 4-B; 5-J; 6-F; 7-D; 8-C; 9-I; 10-E
10. They're cousins.
11. Hank Williams
12. The Crazy Tennesseans—Acuff changed the name after he joined the Grand Ole Opry in 1938, at the suggestion of WSM's George D. Hay and David Stone.
13. Bill Anderson (1960), who wrote the song, followed by Roy Clark (1963, as "Tips of My Fingers"), Eddy Arnold (1966), Jean Shepard (1975), and Steve Wariner (1992, as "The Tips of My Fingers").
14. From his high-school football exploits—He was a running back.
15. The "slip-note" style—so called because Cramer would slip up to the note from the whole tone beneath it.
16. They weren't—Betty Jack Davis and Mary Frances Penick (Skeeter Davis) were best friends in high school.
17. Harold Lloyd Jenkins took his stage name from the towns of Conway, Arkansas, and Twitty, Texas.
18. Singers Cowboy Copas and Hawkshaw Hawkins, along with Randy Hughes, Cline's manager and pilot of the plane.
19. Hungarian composer Béla Bartók.
20. "Oh, Lonesome Me" and "I Can't Stop Loving You"
21. Jim Reeves
22. Ronnie Dunn, but not by much—He had two charting solo singles, both of which peaked at #59—"It's Written All Over Your Face" and "She Put the Sad in All His Songs." Kix Brooks also had two singles that charted—"Baby, When Your Heart Breaks Down" (#73, 1983) and "Sacred Ground" (#87, 1989), which was later revived by McBride & the Ride.

23. The origin of the word "dobro," which describes a type of guitar with metal resonating chambers, is twofold. It derives from the Czechoslovakian word "dobry," meaning good. It also is a contraction of "Dopyera brothers," referring to John and Rudy Dopyera, siblings of Czechoslovakian descent who co-founded the National Guitar Company in 1927.

24. From a one-liner by Groucho Marx on the game show You Bet Your Life.

25. 1-H; 2-B; 3-D; 4-F; 5-I; 6-J; 7-E; 8-C; 9-G; 10-A

26. Noted session guitarist Fred Carter Jr.—who played on such records as Marty Robbins's "El Paso" and Simon & Garfunkel's "The Boxer."

27. "Sing Me Back Home" by Merle Haggard and "Hickory Wind" by Byrds member Gram Parsons. They'd been expected to sing a second Haggard tune, but Parsons switched songs at the last second.

28. Johnny Cash, Waylon Jennings, Kris Kristofferson, and Willie Nelson.

29. Colter, whose given name is Miriam Johnson, took her stage name from her great-great-uncle Jesse Colter, reputed to be a member of the infamous James Gang.

30. He hung an iron doorstop from a coat hanger, then struck the doorstop with a hammer.

31. 1-B; 2-E; 3-G; 4-F; 5-A; 6-C; 7-D

32. Bill Monroe, or William Smith Monroe—"WSM."

33. 1-I; 2-A; 3-D; 4-B; 5-F; 6-E; 7-J; 8-G; 9-H; 10-C

34. "Will the Circle Be Unbroken."

35. "Halley Came to Jackson" and "Dreamland."

36. Three of Loretta's seven siblings got records on the radio—most famously Crystal Gayle, who had more than 50 singles, including "Don't It Make My Brown Eyes Blue" and "Why Have You Left the One You Left Me For." Two younger siblings also placed singles on the charts' lower levels: Peggy Sue, whose biggest hit was 1969's "I'm Dynamite," and Jay Lee Webb, who reached #21 in 1969 with "She's Lookin' Better by the Minute."

37. Waylon Jennings, Willie Nelson, and Kenny Rogers. Several other artists who sang on the record also have had charting country hits, including Kim Carnes, Ray Charles, the Pointer Sisters, and Lionel Richie. USA for Africa's "We Are the World" spent six weeks on the country chart, peaking at #76.

38. When asked about her husband's rumored marital infidelities, Clinton said: "You know, I'm not sitting here as some little woman standing by my man like Tammy Wynette. I am sitting here because I love him and I respect him and I honor what he's been through and what we've been through together. And

you know, if that's not enough for people, then heck, don't vote for him." An infuriated Wynette said that Clinton's statement denigrated "every true country music fan and every person who has 'made it on their own' with no one to take them to a White House." Clinton later called to apologize.

39. Siblings Jim Ed, Maxine, and Bonnie Brown. Sister Norma Brown briefly replaced Jim Ed during his military service.

40. The Glen Campbell Goodtime Hour, 1968–1972.

41. Dave Rowland, Vicki Hackeman, and Jackie Frantz.

42. Parton is one of the owners of Sandollar Productions—a producer of the television show.

43. A.P. Carter; his wife, Sara Carter; and his sister-in-law (and Sara's cousin), Maybelle Carter. Sara's daughter Janette and Maybelle's daughters Anita, Helen, and June performed in later versions of the group.

44. Willie Nelson, Neil Young, and John Mellencamp organized the first Farm Aid concert, which was held September 22, 1985, in Champaign, Illinois. Here's the talent line-up: Alabama • Dave Alvin & the Allnighters • Hoyt Axton • Beach Boys • Bon Jovi • T Bone Burnette • Glen Campbell • Johnny Cash • Jubal Clarke • David Allan Coe • John Conlee • Danny Cooksey • Charlie Daniels Band • John Denver • Bob Dylan • Joe Ely • John Fogerty • Foreigner • Vince Gill • Vern Gosdin • Arlo Guthrie • Sammy Hagar • Merle Haggard • Charlie Haid • Daryl Hall • Emmylou Harris • Don Henley • Timothy Hutton • Waylon Jennings • Billy Joel • George Jones • Rickie Lee Jones • B.B. King • Carole King • Kris Kristofferson • Bobby Krueger • Huey Lewis • Lone Justice • Loretta Lynn • Delbert McClinton • John Mellencamp • Roger Miller • Joni Mitchell • Willie Nelson & Family • Randy Newman • Roy Orbison • Tom Petty • Charley Pride • Bonnie Raitt • Lou Reed • Judy Rodman • Johnny Rodriguez • Kenny Rogers • John Schneider • Brian Setzer • Southern Pacific • Sissy Spacek • Tanya Tucker • Eddie Van Halen • Dottie West • Debra Winger • Winters Brothers • Neil Young

45. 1-F; 2-D; 3-G; 4-B; 5-H; 6-I; 7-E; 8-A; 9-C; 10-J

46. Two—But neither of them are named Statler. Harold and Don Reid are the group's siblings. The Statler name comes from a brand of tissue.

47. 1-H; 2-I; 3-C; 4-O; 5-T; 6-P; 7-J; 8-K; 9-D; 10-L; 11-S; 12-B; 13-E; 14-A; 15-R; 16-N; 17-F; 18-G; 19-M; 20-Q

48. August 28—Twain was born in 1965, Rimes in 1982.

49. "Cry! Cry! Cry!"—which was backed with "Hey Porter." It was released on June 21, 1955.

50. Kris Kristofferson—Kristofferson hosted the show on July 31, 1976, the last episode of SNL's first

season. Garth Brooks, Willie Nelson, and Dolly Parton have also hosted the show, as have Johnny Cash, Ray Charles, Olivia Newton-John, and Rick Nelson.

51. September 8—Howard was born in 1927, Cline in 1932.

52. From comedian Junior Samples's recurring used-car-salesman routine on Hee Haw. Samples would hold up a sign with his phone number, BR5-49.

53. 1-I; 2-R; 3-O; 4-M; 5-E; 6-S; 7-F; 8-J; 9-H; 10-D; 11-T; 12-K; 13-B; 14-P; 15-L; 16-Q; 17-G; 18-N; 19-A; 20-C

54. Sonny James & George Strait—James's 1969 album was called The Astrodome Presents Sonny James; Strait's, released in 2003, was called For the Last Time: Live from the Astrodome.

55. 1-D; 2-I; 3-F; 4-C; 5-E; 6-G; 7-H; 8-A; 9-B

56. Roy Clark and Buck Owens—Owens left the show in 1986.

57. September 25—Cyrus was born in 1961, Messina in 1970.

58. Stonewall Jackson—who claims to be descended from the general.

59. Minnie Pearl

60. Williams's father nicknamed him "Bocephus"—which was also the name of one of Grand Ole Opry comedian Rod Brasfield's ventriloquist dummies.

61. Buddy Jewell—Jewell, 42 when he won, had been a demo singer in Nashville for a decade and also briefly had been a member of the Four Guys.

62. McCall, who had nine Top Forty country hits, including the 1975 smash "Convoy," and the neo-classical instrumental act Mannheim Steamroller are both brainchildren of Chip Davis. Davis and Bill Fries, at the time two Nebraska-based jingle writers, originally created the C.W. McCall character as part of an ad campaign for Old Home Bread. Fries provided McCall's voice; Davis wrote the music. The same year "Convoy" came out, Davis also released the first Mannheim Steamroller album, Fresh Aire I. The two acts "reunited" for the 2003 album American Spirit.

63. Johnny Cash [as a coyote on Season Eight's "El Viaje Misterioso de Nuestro Jomer (The Mysterious Voyage of Homer)"]; Hank Williams Jr. (sang a jingle for the fictitious Canyonero SUV in Season Nine's "The Last Temptation of Krust"); Dolly Parton (as herself, in Season Ten's "Sunday, Cruddy Sunday"); and Willie Nelson (as himself, in Season Eleven's "Behind the Laughter"). Other Simpsons guests, such as Terry Cashman, David Crosby, Tom Jones, Kid Rock, Linda Ronstadt, Ringo Starr, Sting, and James Taylor, have also appeared on the country charts [in some form or another.]

64. 1-A; 2-E; 3-J; 4-G; 5-I; 6-C; 7-H; 8-D; 9-F; 10-B

65. Payne, a black street musician who lived in Greenville, Alabama, was one of Hank Williams's formative musical influences. Williams shined shoes and sold newspapers so he could pay Payne for guitar lessons.

66. "Death cannot kill what never dies."

67. Felice & Boudleaux Bryant—The husband-and-wife team had some 1,500 songs recorded during their career, including Eddy Arnold's "How's the World Treating You," Roy Orbison's "Love Hurts," Bob Luman's "Let's Think About Living," and a dozen Everly Brothers hits, including "Wake Up, Little Susie" and "All I Have to Do Is Dream."

68. Lisa Hartman first came to prominence playing Tabitha Stevens, the daughter of Bewitched's Samantha and Darren Stevens, in the 1977 spin-off series Tabitha.

69. Gram Parsons

70. Hot Band, Nash Ramblers, and Spyboy.

71. "Where's the Dress," by Moe Bandy & Joe Stampley

72. A black Lexus LX470 sport-utility vehicle.

73. Tommy Collins—whose real name was Leonard Sipes. Collins wrote the Haggard hits "Sam Hill," "Carolyn," and "The Roots of My Raising."

74. 1-C; 2-G; 3-F; 4-H; 5-B; 6-A; 7-D; 8-E

75. Cyndi Thomson

76. 1-B; 2-J; 3-I; 4-D; 5-C; 6-G; 7-H; 8-A; 9-E; 10-F

77. "Where are your guts?"

78. 1-A; 2-G; 3-B; 4-D; 5-H; 6-E; 7-F; 8-C

79. Doug Sahm—who would later record with the Texas Tornados, appeared on the magazine's December 7, 1968 cover. But Elvis Presley, who had significantly more charting country singles than Sahm, was the cover subject for the July 12, 1969 issue.

80. Del Reeves—who had one charting single for the label: "The Only Girl I Can't Forget" (#13, 1963). Reeves's breakthrough hit came two years later with "Girl on the Billboard," for United Artists.

81. Charley Pride (Super Bowl VIII), Garth Brooks (Super Bowl XXVII), Faith Hill (Super Bowl XXXIC), and Dixie Chicks (Super Bowl XXXVII). Aaron Neville, Neil Diamond, and Jewel also have both charted country records and sung the national anthem at the Super Bowl.

82. Harrison Ford

83. Jerry & Tammy Sullivan—Griggs also married Jerry's daughter Stephanie.

84. Kix Brooks

85. Johnny Cash—Orbison, fortunately and to his credit, did neither.

86. Kris Kristofferson—The former Air Force captain borrowed the helicopter from the Tennessee National Guard.

87. 1-E; 2-H; 3-G; 4-A; 5-I; 6-B; 7-F; 8-J; 9-D; 10-C

88. Cline last performed on March 3, 1963, at a Kansas City benefit concert for the family of DJ "Cactus" Jack Call, who had died in a car accident. Hawkshaw Hawkins, Cowboy Copas, Wilma Lee and Stoney Cooper, George Jones, Billy Walker, and Dottie West were also on the bill.

89. Onstage during a show in London, Ontario—before a crowd of 5,000 people. They were married March 1, 1968.

90. 1-G; 2-I; 3-B; 4-D; 5-C; 6-E; 7-F; 8-A; 9-H

91. 1-G; 2-A; 3-F; 4-D; 5-H; 6-C; 7-B; 8-E

92. 1-J; 2-C; 3-F; 4-B; 5-G; 6-E; 7-A; 8-D; 9-I; 10-H

93. 1-C; 2-A; 3-B; 4-E; 5-F; 6-G; 7-I; 8-H; 9-D

94. 1-A; 2-G; 3-D; 4-E; 5-C; 6-B; 7-F

95. 1-E; 2-F; 3-B; 4-L; 6-H; 7-G; 8-J; 9-C; 10-D

96. 1-A; 2-F; 3-L; 4-H; 5-D; 6-I; 7-K; 8-C; 9-B; 10-J; 11-G; 12-E

97. 1-E; 2-A; 3-F; 4-C; 5-D; 6-K; 7-J; 8-I; 9-L; 10-B; 11-H; 12-G

98. Patsy Cline

99. "Shania" is an Ojibway Indian name that roughly translates as "I'm on my way."

100. Tug McGraw—a pitcher for the New York Mets and Philadelphia Phillies between 1965 and 1984.

101. Dwight Yoakam

102. John Schneider—aka "Bo Duke." Schneider's 13 Top Forty records included the chart-topping "I've Been around Enough to Know" and "What's a Memory Like You (Doing in a Love like This)?" Tom ("Luke Duke") Wopat hit the Top Forty seven times, but never reached the Top Ten.

103. Loretta Young—who appeared in such films as *Kentucky*, *The Farmer's Daughter*, and *The Bishop's Wife*.

104. Roger Dean Miller was named for a pair of Hall of Famers who spent much of their careers with the St. Louis Cardinals, second baseman Rogers Hornsby and pitcher Dizzy Dean.

105. June 26, 1977, in Indianapolis, Indiana—Presley died less than two months later.

106. 1-N; 2-R; 3-C; 4-O; 5-H; 6-Q; 7-L; 8-P; 9-J; 10-K; 11-E; 12-D; 13-M; 14-F; 15-G; 16-S; 17-B; 18-A; 19-T; 20-I

NAME
THAT
SONG

1. **What is the only Charlie Daniels record to top either the *Billboard* country or pop charts?**
   A) "In America"
   B) "Long-Haired Country Boy"
   C) "The Devil Went Down to Georgia"
   D) "The South's Gonna Do It Again"

2. **The following four records all made *Billboard* country, pop, and r&b charts during the 1950s, but only one reached the top spot on all three charts. Which one?**
   A) "Be-Bop-A-Lula," Gene Vincent
   B) "Blue Suede Shoes," Carl Perkins
   C) "Don't Be Cruel," Elvis Presley
   D) "Whole Lot of Shakin' Going On," Jerry Lee Lewis

3. **Lonestar had a hit with which of these songs?**
   A) "I'm Already There"
   B) "Let Me Be There"
   C) "There's Been a Change in Me"
   D) "There You'll Be"

4. **What song by rock band Kiss did Garth Brooks cover for a 1994 Kiss tribute album?**
   A) "Lick It Up"   B) "Calling Dr. Love"   C) "Hard Luck Woman"   D) "Beth"

5. **What Tammy Wynette hit begins with the line, "Sometimes it's hard to be a woman"?**
   A) "Your Good Girl's Gonna Go Bad"
   B) "Woman to Woman"
   C) "'Til I Get It Right"
   D) "Stand by Your Man"

6. **What 1971 smash hit begins with the lines, "Take the ribbon from my hair/Shake it loose and let it fall"?**
   A) "After the Fire Is Gone," Conway Twitty & Loretta Lynn
   B) "Good Lovin' (Makes It Right)," Tammy Wynette
   C) "Help Me Make It through the Night," Sammi Smith
   D) "You're My Man," Lynn Anderson

7. **The "Earl" character the Dixie Chicks kill off in "Goodbye Earl" appears in another artist's Top Forty single, also penned by Dennis Linde. Which one?**
   A) "Bubba Shot the Jukebox," Mark Chesnutt
   B) "Callin' Baton Rouge," Garth Brooks
   C) "John Deere Green," Joe Diffie
   D) "Queen of My Double Wide Trailer," Sammy Kershaw

*Answers begin on page 169.

8. **What was the first bluegrass song to reach #1 on the *Billboard* country charts?**
   A) "Dueling Banjos," Eric Weissberg & Steve Mandell
   B) "Foggy Mountain Breakdown," Flatt & Scruggs
   C) "I Am a Man of Constant Sorrow," Soggy Bottom Boys
   D) "The Ballad of Jed Clampett," Flatt & Scruggs

9. **What song was a two-time #1 in 1949, first for Ernest Tubb, then for Margaret Whiting and Jimmy Wakely?**
   A) "I Love You So Much It Hurts"
   B) "Don't Rob Another Man's Castle"
   C) "Slipping Around"
   D) "Candy Kisses"

10. **With what song, usually associated with Elvis Presley, did Willie Nelson and Leon Russell top the country charts in 1979?**
    A) "Are You Lonesome Tonight?"
    B) "Can't Help Falling in Love"
    C) "Don't Be Cruel"
    D) "Heartbreak Hotel"

11. **What Dolly Parton and Kenny Rogers duet topped both the country and the pop charts in 1983?**
    A) "Every Time Two Fools Collide"
    B) "What Are We Doin' in Love?"
    C) "Islands in the Stream"
    D) "Real Love"

Kenny Rogers

12. **In what song did Bill Monroe pay tribute to one of his relatives, old-time fiddler Pendleton Vandiver?**
    A) "Blue Grass Breakdown"   C) "Wheel Hoss"
    B) "Goodbye Old Pal"   D) "Uncle Pen"

13. **Which of these records was Dan Fogelberg's sole Top Forty country hit?**
    A) "Part of the Plan"   C) "Down the Road Mountain Pass"
    B) "Same Old Lang Syne"   D) "Leader of the Band"

Answers begin on page 169.

14. **Which song gave former Creedence Clearwater Revival leader John Fogerty his only Top Forty country hit?**
    A) "Big Train (from Memphis)"
    B) "The Old Man Down the Road"
    C) "Rock and Roll Girls"
    D) "Rockin' All Over the World"

15. **On April 19, 1980, women held the top five positions on *Billboard's* country chart for the first time in history, with records by Debby Boone, Crystal Gayle, Emmylou Harris, Dottie West, and Tammy Wynette. Which single held the top slot?**
    A) "It's Like We Never Said Goodbye," Crystal Gayle
    B) "A Lesson in Leavin'," Dottie West
    C) "Are You on the Road to Lovin' Me Again," Debby Boone
    D) "Beneath Still Waters," Emmylou Harris

16. **What was Willie Nelson's first Top Forty duet hit?**
    A) "Willingly," with Shirley Collie
    B) "After the Fire Is Gone," with Tracy Nelson
    C) "Good Hearted Woman," with Waylon Jennings
    D) "Lily Dale," with Darrell McCall

17. **What was the first #1 country hit by a solo female singer?**
    A) "I Let the Stars Get in My Eyes," Goldie Hill
    B) "I'll Never Be Free," Kay Starr
    C) "It Wasn't God Who Made Honky Tonk Angels," Kitty Wells
    D) "A Dear John Letter," Jean Shepard

18. **What was the last song Hank Williams recorded at his final recording session, on September 23, 1952?**
    A) "I Could Never Be Ashamed of You"
    B) "Your Cheatin' Heart"
    C) "Kaw-Liga"
    D) "Take These Chains from My Heart"

19. **What Ben E. King pop hit did Mickey Gilley remake for the *Urban Cowboy* soundtrack and take to #1 in 1980?**
    A) "Don't Play that Song (You Lied)"
    B) "I (Who Have Nothing)"
    C) "Spanish Harlem"
    D) "Stand by Me"

20. **What Bobbie Gentry song was later also a hit for Reba McEntire?**
    A) "Ode to Billie Joe"
    B) "Little Rock"
    C) "Fancy"
    D) "The Night the Lights Went Out in Georgia"

Answers begin on page 169.

21. **Which of these country-pop crossover hits from the late 1960s did not top the pop charts?**
    A) "Ode to Billie Joe," Bobbie Gentry
    B) "Honey," Bobby Goldsboro
    C) "Stand by Your Man," Tammy Wynette
    D) "Harper Valley P.T.A.," Jeannie C. Riley

22. **What was the first hit for Monument Records?**
    A) "Gotta Travel On," Billy Grammer
    B) "Only the Lonely (Know the Way I Feel)," Roy Orbison
    C) "Yakety Sax," Boots Randolph
    D) "There's Your Trouble," Dixie Chicks

23. **What Jim Reeves hit begins, "Put your sweet lips a little closer to the phone"?**
    A) "Am I Losing You"
    B) "He'll Have to Go"
    C) "I Won't Come in While He's There"
    D) "Welcome to My World"

24. **What Shenandoah hit featuring Alison Krauss on vocals, won a Country Music Association award for Vocal Event of the Year?**
    A) "Ghost in This House"
    B) "Next to You, Next to Me"
    C) "Mama Knows"
    D) "Somewhere in the Vicinity of the Heart"

25. **What holiday classic was a Top Ten hit for Ernest Tubb for three consecutive years?**
    A) "Blue Christmas"
    B) "Here Comes Santa Claus (Down Santa Claus Lane)"
    C) "Pretty Paper"
    D) "Will Santy Come to Shanty Town"

26. **What Bill Anderson song topped the charts for both Ray Price and Mickey Gilley?**
    A) "City Lights"
    B) "Crazy Arms"
    C) "Heartaches by the Number"
    D) "Make the World Go Away"

27. **What song was a hit for both Johnny Cash and his daughter Rosanne Cash?**
    A) "Ballad of a Teenage Queen"
    B) "Guess Things Happen That Way"
    C) "Tennessee Flat Top Box"
    D) "Train of Love"

28. **What Rodney Crowell song did Lee Ann Womack take up the country charts in 2001— 21 years after it had been a Top Forty pop hit for its writer?**
    A) "Ashes by Now"
    B) "I Hope You Dance"
    C) "Does My Ring Burn Your Finger?"
    D) "Why They Call It Falling"

Answers begin on page 169.

29. What song did Willie Nelson turn into a chart-topping, award-winning single after it had already been a hit for both Elvis Presley and John Wesley Ryles?

A) "Always on My Mind"
B) "Help Me Make It through the Night"
C) "Heartbreak Hotel"
D) "Living in the Promiseland"

Faith Hill

30. What Faith Hill hit previously had been recorded by 1960s rock singer Janis Joplin?

A) "Love Ain't Like That"
B) "Piece of My Heart"
C) "This Kiss"
D) "Wild One"

31. What song was a hit for Johnny Cash in 1955 and for his one-time sideman Marty Stuart in 1989?

A) "Cry! Cry! Cry!"
B) "Get Rhythm"
C) "Home of the Blues"
D) "There You Go"

32. What song was a Top Forty hit for Jim Reeves twice before Ronnie Milsap took it to the top of the charts in 1981?

A) "Am I Losing You"
B) "Any Day Now"
C) "I Wouldn't Have Missed It for the World"
D) "(There's) No Gettin' over Me"

33. What song topped the charts in 1952 for both Slim Willet and Skeets McDonald?

A) "Don't Let the Stars Get in Your Eyes"
B) "The Wild Side of Life"
C) "Give Me More, More, More (of Your Kisses)"
D) "Back Street Affair"

34. What song hit the charts twice for Johnny Cash, first in 1956, then, with a live recording, in 1968?

A) "A Boy Named Sue"
B) "Folsom Prison Blues"
C) "I Walk the Line"
D) "Ring of Fire"

35. Which Hank Williams song became a #1 hit only when his son recorded it?

A) "Honky Tonk Blues"
B) "Honky Tonkin'"
C) "Kaw-Liga"
D) "Long Gone Lonesome Blues"

Answers begin on page 169.

36. **What song was a #3 solo hit for Waylon Jennings in 1972 but turned into a chart-topping Country Music Association Single of the Year when he recut it with Willie Nelson?**
    A) "Good Hearted Woman"
    B) "I've Always Been Crazy"
    C) "Mammas Don't Let Your Babies Grow Up to Be Cowboys"
    D) "Luckenbach, Texas (Back to the Basics of Love)"

37. **Which of these Kenny Chesney hits was inspired by a line from the 1996 film *Jerry Maguire*?**
    A) "All I Need to Know"   C) "She Thinks My Tractor's Sexy"
    B) "How Forever Feels"   D) "You Had Me from Hello"

38. **Which Buck Owens hit, written by Johnny Russell and Voni Morrison, was covered by the Beatles?**
    A) "Above and Beyond"   C) "Before You Go"
    B) "Act Naturally"   D) "My Heart Skips a Beat"

39. **These four Elvis Presley singles hit #1 on *Billboard*'s country singles charts in 1956. Which one topped the charts first?**
    A) "Heartbreak Hotel"   C) "I Forgot to Remember to Forget"
    B) "Hound Dog"   D) "I Want You, I Need You, I Love You"

40. **What was Toby Keith's first #1 *Billboard* country single?**
    A) "Should've Been a Cowboy"
    B) "Who's That Man"
    C) "How Do You Like Me Now?!"
    D) "Courtesy of the Red, White and Blue (the Angry American)"

41. **What Trisha Yearwood single first topped *Billboard's* country chart?**
    A) "She's in Love with the Boy"   C) "The Song Remembers When"
    B) "Wrong Side of Memphis"   D) "Thinkin' about You"

42. **Which Dolly Parton song did Whitney Houston record for the soundtrack of her 1992 film, *The Bodyguard*?**
    A) "Baby I'm Burnin'"   C) "The Last One To Touch Me"
    B) "I Will Always Love You"   D) "Light of a Clear Blue Morning"

*Answers begin on page 169.

43. **What song was a chart-topping duet for Reba McEntire and Linda Davis?**
A) "Does He Love You"
B) "If You See Him"
C) "That Makes Two of Us"
D) "The Heart Won't Lie"

44. **From which of Gene Watson's hits did his band take its name?**
A) "Love in the Hot Afternoon"
B) "Paper Rosie"
C) "Farewell Party"
D) "Fourteen Carat Mind"

45. **What Hank Williams song starts with the lines, "Hear that lonesome whippoorwill?/He sounds too blue to fly"?**
A) "I'll Never Get Out of This World Alive"
B) "I'm So Lonesome I Could Cry"
C) "Lonesome Whistle"
D) "Moanin' the Blues"

46. **Which Garth Brooks hit starts with the line, "Blame it all on my roots, I showed up in boots and ruined your black-tie affair"?**
A) "Ain't Going Down ('til the Sun Comes Up)"
B) "The Dance"
C) "Friends in Low Places"
D) "Shameless"

47. **What Alan Jackson hit begins with the line, "Cowboys don't cry, and heroes don't die"?**
A) "Here in the Real World"
B) "Someday"
C) "Wanted"
D) "(Who Says) You Can't Have It All"

48. **The line "From the great Atlantic Ocean to the wide Pacific shore" begins which classic train song?**
A) "Fireball Mail"
B) "Orange Blossom Special"
C) "Wabash Cannon Ball"
D) "Waiting for a Train"

49. **What country music tale begins "On a warm summer's evening, on a train bound for nowhere"?**
A) "Coward of the County"
B) "The Gambler"
C) "Lucille"
D) "Sweet Music Man"

50. **What coal-mining classic starts with the line, "Some people say a man is made out of mud"?**
A) "Big Bad John" B) "Dark as a Dungeon" C) "Miner's Prayer" D) "Sixteen Tons"

*Answers begin on page 169.

51. **What song begins, "In 1814 we took a little trip/Along with Colonel Jackson down the mighty Mississip'"?**
    A) "The Ballad of Ira Hayes"
    B) "The Battle of New Orleans"
    C) "Bonaparte's Retreat"
    D) "Soldier's Joy"

52. **What Glen Campbell hit starts with the lines, "It's knowing that your door is always open and your path is free to walk/That makes me tend to leave my sleeping bag rolled up and stashed behind your couch"?**
    A) "By the Time I Get to Phoenix"
    B) "Dreams of the Everyday Housewife"
    C) "Galveston"
    D) "Gentle on My Mind"

53. **Which song by 1960s pop group the Monkees did Anne Murray turn into a country hit?**
    A) "Last Train to Clarksville"
    B) "I'm a Believer"
    C) "A Little Bit Me, a Little Bit You"
    D) "Daydream Believer"

54. **Which Aerosmith song did Garth Brooks transform into a country hit?**
    A) "Dream On"
    B) "The Fever"
    C) "I Don't Want to Miss a Thing"
    D) "Cryin'"

55. **What Patsy Cline classic did Garth Brooks revive on his album *The Chase*?**
    A) "Crazy"
    B) "Leavin' on Your Mind"
    C) "I Fall to Pieces"
    D) "Walkin' after Midnight"

56. **What song did Toby Keith record with rock singer Sting?**
    A) "Dream Walkin'"
    B) "Getcha Some"
    C) "I'm So Happy I Can't Stop Crying"
    D) "Who's That Man"

57. **On what song did Eagles member Don Henley sing with Trisha Yearwood?**
    A) "Down on My Knees"
    B) "Walkaway Joe"
    C) "Wrong Side of Memphis"
    D) "You Say You Will"

58. **What was the first Faith Hill/Tim McGraw duet to hit the charts?**
    A) "Angry All the Time"
    B) "It's Your Love"
    C) "Just to Hear You Say That You Love Me"
    D) "Let's Make Love"

59. **What was Alan Jackson's first single?**
    A) "Blue Blooded Woman"
    B) "Chasin' That Neon Rainbow"
    C) "Here in the Real World"
    D) "Wanted"

Answers begin on page 169.

60. Which Bob Dylan song did Garth Brooks take to the top of the country charts?

A) "Blowin' in the Wind"
B) "Forever Young"
C) "'Til I Fell in Love with You"
D) "To Make You Feel My Love"

61. According to its own lyrics, what is "the perfect country & western song"?

A) "Family Tradition"
B) "It's Hard to Be Humble"
C) "Put Some Drive in Your Country"
D) "You Never Even Called Me by My Name"

62. What was the first Garth Brooks single to top the *Billboard* country chart

A) "Much Too Young (to Feel This Damn Old)"?
B) "If Tomorrow Never Comes"
C) "The Dance"
D) "Friends in Low Places"

63. What Freddie Hart song won Song of the Year honors from both the Academy of Country Music and the Country Music Association in 1971?

A) "Bless Your Heart"
B) "Easy Loving"
C) "Got the All Overs for You (All over Me)"
D) "My Hang-Up Is You"

64. What Bill Monroe song brought the Kentucky HeadHunters to the country charts in 1989?

A) "Blue Moon of Kentucky"
B) "Mule Skinner Blues"
C) "Cry, Cry Darlin'"
D) "Walk Softly on This Heart of Mine"

65. What song did Merle Haggard write as a tribute to Elvis Presley?

A) "The Emptiest Arms in the World"
B) "From Graceland to the Promised Land"
C) "The King Is Gone"
D) "The Temptiest Arms in the World"

66. Which chart-topping Willie Nelson single begins, "In the twilight glow I see her"?

A) "Always on My Mind"
B) "Angel Flying Too Close to the Ground"
C) "Blue Eyes Crying in the Rain"
D) "Blue Skies"

67. What Little Jimmy Dickens hit did late-night talk-show host Johnny Carson inspire?

A) "Take an Old Cold 'Tater (and Wait)"
B) "Out Behind the Barn"
C) "May the Bird of Paradise Fly up Your Nose"
D) "(You've Been Quite a Doll) Raggedy Ann"

*Answers begin on page 169.

68. Which Johnny Cash & June Carter duet begins, "We got married in a fever, hotter than a pepper sprout"?

A) "It Ain't Me, Babe"   C) "If I Were a Carpenter"

B) "Jackson"   D) "Old Time Feeling"

69. A cover of what George Jones hit became Patty Loveless's first Top Ten single?

A) "If My Heart Had Windows" C) "Walk Through This World with Me"

B) "A Picture of Me without You" D) "The Window Up Above"

70. Which of Alan Jackson's hits was co-written by Randy Travis?

A) "Chattahoochee"

B) "Midnight in Montgomery"

C) "Mercury Blues"

D) "She's Got the Rhythm (and I Got the Blues)"

Alan Jackson

71. What was Shania Twain's first #1 single?

A) "Any Man of Mine"

B) "Whose Bed Have Your Boots Been Under?"

C) "(If You're Not in It for Love) I'm Outta Here"

D) "You Win My Love"

72. Though he was scheduled to sing only his hit "Pop a Top," what song did Alan Jackson break into during his performance at the *1999 Country Music Association Awards Show*?

A) "Chattahoochee"   C) "Who's Gonna Fill Their Shoes"

B) "Summertime Blues"   D) "Choices"

73. What Tommy Collins tune was a hit for both Faron Young and George Strait?

A) "The Chair"   C) "Let's Fall to Pieces Together"

B) "If You Ain't Lovin' (You Ain't Livin')" D) "Right or Wrong"

74. What Willie Nelson hit contains the lines, "Good morning, America, how are you? Don't you know me? I'm your native son"?

A) "Bloody Mary Morning"   C) "Living in the Promiseland"

B) "City of New Orleans"   D) "On the Road Again"

Answers begin on page 169.

75. **What Hank Williams song begins, "I tried so hard, my dear, to show that you're my ev'ry dream"?**
   A) "Cold, Cold Heart"
   B) "Crazy Heart"
   C) "I Can't Help It (If I'm Still in Love with You)"
   D) "Your Cheatin' Heart"

76. **Which of Merle Haggard's singles begins, "I raised a lot of Cain in my younger days, while Mama used to pray my crops would fail"?**
   A) "(I'm a Lonesome) Fugitive"   C) "Mama's Hungry Eyes"
   B) "Mama Tried"   D) "Swinging Doors"

77. **What famous ballad of murder and infidelity begins with the lines, "Ten years ago, on a cold, dark night/Someone was killed 'neath the town hall light"?**
   A) "Carroll County Accident"   C) "The Night the Lights Went Out in Georgia"
   B) "The Long Black Veil"   D) "Tom Dooley"

78. **What was the first Loretta Lynn single to top the *Billboard* country chart?**
   A) "I'm a Honky Tonk Girl"
   B) "You Ain't Woman Enough"
   C) "Don't Come Home A' Drinkin' (with Lovin' on Your Mind)"
   D) "Coal Miner's Daughter"

79. **Which Faith Hill hit did Alan Jackson write?**
   A) "I Can't Do That Anymore"   C) "Love Ain't Like That"
   B) "It Matters to Me"   D) "Take Me As I Am"

80. **Cartoon producer Hanna-Barbera forced a change in the title of which George Jones hit?**
   A) "The Bird"   C) "The King Is Gone (So Are You)"
   B) "I Don't Need Your Rockin' Chair" D) "High-Tech Redneck"

81. **Which of these songs did not win the Country Music Association's Song of the Year award two consecutive years?**
   A) "Always on My Mind"   C) "He Stopped Loving Her Today"
   B) "Easy Loving"   D) "Murder on Music Row"

82. **What famous Cajun song did Waylon Jennings record for his first single?**
   A) "Big Mamou"   B) "Diggy Diggy Lo"   C) "Jambalaya"   D) "Jole Blon"

Answers begin on page 169.

83. Which Stonewall Jackson hit topped the country charts for five weeks in 1959 and even crossed into the pop Top Five?

A) "Life to Go"

B) "Smoke along the Track"

C) "Waterloo"

D) "B.J. the D.J."

84. What was the first Dolly Parton single to cross over to the pop Top Forty?

A) "I Will Always Love You"

B) "Love Is Like a Butterfly"

C) "Here You Come Again"

D) "Baby I'm Burnin'"

85. Which of these Alan Jackson hits did Tom T. Hall write?

A) "Gone Country"

B) "Little Bitty"

C) "Tall, Tall Trees"

D) "Tonight I Climbed the Wall"

86. George Hamilton IV first hit on the pop side in 1956 with "A Rose and a Baby Ruth," but his only #1 country hit came several years later. What was it?

A) "Abilene"

B) "Break My Mind"

C) "Truck Driving Man"

D) "She's a Little Bit Country"

87. What song did Lefty Frizzell write from jail as an apology to his wife?

A) "Don't Stay Away (till Love Grows Cold)"

B) "I Love You a Thousand Ways"

C) "Look What Thoughts Will Do"

D) "I Want to Be with You Always"

88. What Patsy Cline record hit the charts after she performed the song on *Arthur Godfrey's Talent Scouts* TV show in January 1957?

A) "Crazy"

B) "There He Goes"

C) "Just Out of Reach (of My Two Open Arms)"

D) "Walkin' after Midnight"

89. What was Merle Haggard's first #1 single?

A) "Sing a Sad Song"

B) "Swinging Doors"

C) "The Bottle Let Me Down"

D) "The Fugitive"

90. What was George Jones's first #1 single?

A) "Why Baby Why"

B) "Color of the Blues"

C) "White Lightning"

D) "The Window up Above"

91. What was Johnny Cash's first #1 record?

A) "Cry! Cry! Cry!"

B) "So Doggone Lonesome"

C) "Folsom Prison Blues"

D) "I Walk the Line"

*Answers begin on page 169.

Eddy Arnold

92. **What song, originally a hit for Eddy Arnold, begins with the line, "You give your hand to me, and then you say hello"?**
    A) "Anytime"
    B) "I Really Don't Want to Know"
    C) "Take Me in Your Arms and Hold Me"
    D) "You Don't Know Me"

93. **In 2001, Brad Paisley and Patty Loveless both released versions of a Darrell Scott song about coal mining. What was it?**
    A) "Out of Control Raging Fire"
    B) "Sorrowful Angels"
    C) "Two Feet of Topsoil"
    D) "You'll Never Leave Harlan Alive"

94. **What Roy Acuff hit led to his joining the Grand Ole Opry?**
    A) "Fireball Mail"   C) "Wabash Cannonball"
    B) "The Great Speckled Bird"   D) "The Wreck on the Highway"

95. **Alan Jackson debuted this song on the *2001 Country Music Association Awards Show*. It won Song of the Year in 2002. What was the song?**
    A) "Drive"
    B) "Where Were You (When the World Stopped Turning)"
    C) "Work in Progress"
    D) "Murder on Music Row"

96. **Glen Campbell took two records to #1 on both the pop and country charts. The first was "Rhinestone Cowboy." What was the other?**
    A) "Country Boy (You Got Your Feet in L.A.)"   C) "Sunflower"
    B) "Southern Nights"   D) "Wichita Lineman"

97. **What Dixie Chicks record was sitting at #1 when lead singer Natalie Maines told a London audience, "We're ashamed the president of the United States is from Texas," shortly before the U.S. attacked Iraq in March 2003?**
    A) "Long Time Gone"   C) "Travelin' Soldier"
    B) "Landslide"   D) "Truth No. 2"

Answers begin on page 169.

98. Trisha Yearwood and LeAnn Rimes both released versions of what song in 1997?
A) "Everybody Knows"
B) "How Do I Live"
C) "I Need You"
D) "The Light in Your Eyes"

99. What 1973 Charlie Rich record hit #1 on both the country and pop charts?
A) "Behind Closed Doors"
B) "The Most Beautiful Girl"
C) "There Won't Be Anymore"
D) "A Very Special Love Song"

100. What 1981 Eddie Rabbitt single topped the country and the pop charts?
A) "Every Which Way But Loose"
B) "Drivin' My Life Away"
C) "I Love a Rainy Night"
D) "Step by Step"

101. What bluegrass instrumental, played by banjo player Eric Weissberg and guitarist Steve Mandell, became a hit single after being used in the 1972 film *Deliverance*?
A) "Dueling Banjos"
B) "Fire on the Mountain"
C) "Foggy Mountain Breakdown"
D) "Mountain Dew"

102. What chart-topping Lefty Frizzell hit of 1950 was subsequently a #1 hit for Willie Nelson in 1976?
A) "If You've Got the Money I've Got the Time"
B) "I Love You a Thousand Ways"
C) "Always Late (with Your Kisses)"
D) "I Want to Be with You Always"

103. In late 1956, what song was simultaneously a #1 country hit for Marty Robbins and a #1 pop hit for Guy Mitchell?
A) "Ninety-Nine Years (Dead or Alive)"
B) "Maybelline"
C) "A White Sport Coat (and a Pink Carnation)"
D) "Singing the Blues"

104. What Jimmy Dean single topped both the country and the pop charts in the fall of 1961?
A) "Big Bad John"   B) "The Cajun Queen"   C) "Little Black Book"   D) "P.T. 109"

105. What Lionel Richie tune gave Kenny Rogers a chart-topping crossover hit in 1980?
A) "Lady"
B) "Love the World Away"
C) "Lucille"
D) "She Believes in Me"

106. What movie theme was a chart-topping pop and country hit for Dolly Parton in 1981?
A) "Heartbreaker"
B) "But You Know I Love You"
C) "I Will Always Love You"
D) "9 to 5"

*Answers begin on page 169.

107. What Randy Travis record stiffed when first released in 1985, only to top the charts the following year?

A) "1982"

B) "On the Other Hand"

C) "Diggin' Up Bones"

D) "No Place Like Home"

108. What record, that referenced the 1986 explosion of the space shuttle Challenger, was the #1 country song when the space shuttle Columbia disintegrated on February 1, 2003?

A) "Man to Man," Gary Allan

B) "The Baby," Blake Shelton

C) "Have You Forgotten," Darryl Worley

D) "19 Somethin'," Mark Wills

109. What record topped both the pop and country charts for Sonny James in early 1957?

A) "First Date, First Kiss, First Love"

B) "Uh-Huh—mm"

C) "You're the Reason I'm in Love"

D) "Young Love"

110. What song brought the Tractors to the country audience's attention in 1994?

A) "Baby Likes to Rock It"

B) "Shortenin' Bread"

C) "I Wouldn't Tell You No Lie"

D) "Tryin' to Get to New Orleans"

111. What song provided the title for the 1985 Patsy Cline biopic starring Jessica Lange?

A) "Always"

B) "Crazy"

C) "I Fall to Pieces"

D) "Sweet Dreams (of You)"

112. What Tennessee Ernie Ford record topped both the country and the pop charts in late 1955?

A) "Ballad of Davy Crockett"

B) "Mule Train"

C) "Sixteen Tons"

D) "The Shot Gun Boogie"

113. What song won Cal Smith the Country Music Association's Single of the Year award in 1974?

A) "I've Found Someone of My Own"

B) "The Lord Knows I'm Drinking"

C) "Country Bumpkin"

D) "It's Time to Pay the Fiddler"

114. What song, a 1954 hit for both Slim Whitman and Doris Day, did Freddy Fender revive 21 years later and take to the top of the country charts?

A) "Before the Next Teardrop Falls"

B) "Secret Love"

C) "Since I Met You Baby"

D) "Vaya con Dios"

Answers begin on page 169.

115. Which of Garth Brooks's hits did pop singer Billy Joel write?
A) "Unanswered Prayers"　　　　　C) "That Summer"
B) "We Shall Be Free"　　　　　　D) "Shameless"

116. Anne Murray switched the gender on which George Jones classic and made it a #1 country hit for the second time?
A) "[She] He Thinks I Still Care"
B) "[She] He Stopped Loving Her [Him] Today"
C) "A Girl [Guy] I Used to Know"
D) "She's [He's] My Rock"

117. Connie Smith's only #1 hit was her first single. What was it?
A) "Ain't Had No Lovin'"　　　　　C) "Once a Day"
B) "Just One Time"　　　　　　　D) "The Hurtin's All Over"

118. Dean Dillon, one of George Strait's favorite sources of material, had a Top Thirty hit with one of his own songs in 1981. Five years later, Strait took it to the top of the charts. What was it?
A) "Marina Del Rey"
B) "Famous Last Words of a Fool"
C) "Nobody in His Right Mind Would've Left Her"
D) "Ocean Front Property"

119. In what 1969 song did Merle Haggard sing about interracial love?
A) "Carolyn"　　　　　　　　　C) "Sidewalks of Chicago"
B) "Irma Jackson"　　　　　　　D) "The Fightin' Side of Me"

120. In what song does Jerry Reed sing about a poacher who "could trap the biggest, the meanest alligator and just use one hand"?
A) "Alabama Wild Man"　　　　　C) "Ko-Ko Joe"
B) "Amos Moses"　　　　　　　D) "When You're Hot, You're Hot"

121. Kitty Wells's "It Wasn't God Who Made Honky Tonk Angels" is probably the best-known "answer record" in country music history. Which other answer record(s) did Wells release?
A) "Paying for that Back Street Affair"　　　C) "(I'll Always Be Your) Fraulein"
B) "Hey Joe"　　　　　　　　　　　　　D) All of the above

Answers begin on page 169.

122. Tammy Wynette's first #1 record came as a duet with David Houston. What was it?

A) "It's All Over"   C) "I'll Take My Chances with You"

B) "My Elusive Dreams"   D) "Set Me Free"

123. Waylon Jennings and Willie Nelson revived which Ed Bruce hit and took it to the top of the country singles chart in 1978?

A) "Good Hearted Woman"

B) "Just to Satisfy You"

C) "Mammas Don't Let Your Babies Grow Up to Be Cowboys"

D) "Take It to the Limit"

124. What 1955 chart-topping r&b hit for Johnny Ace was later a charting country record for Elvis Presley, Emmylou Harris, and Billy Thunderkloud?

A) "My Song"   C) "Pledging My Love"

B) "Please Forgive Me"   D) "Saving My Love for You"

125. What Amazing Rhythm Aces song, a #11 hit for the group in 1975, did Sammy Kershaw revive in 1994?

A) "Third-Rate Romance"

B) "Amazing Grace (Used to Be Her Favorite Song)"

C) "The End Is Not in Sight (the Cowboy Tune)"

D) "Chevy Van"

126. What Platters song of the 1950s has been a charting country hit for Freddie Hart, Reba McEntire, the Statler Brothers, and Travis Tritt?

A) "Only You (and You Alone)"   C) "Smoke Gets in Your Eyes"

B) "The Great Pretender"   D) "One in a Million"

127. What record earned pianist Del Wood the distinction of being the first female instrumentalist to sell a million copies of a record?

A) "Are You from Dixie?"   C) "Piano Roll Blues"

B) "Down Yonder"   D) "Under the Double Eagle"

128. What was B.J. Thomas's first country hit?

A) "I'm So Lonesome I Could Cry"

B) "Raindrops Keep Falling on My Head"

C) "(Hey Won't You Play) Another Somebody Done Somebody Wrong Song"

D) "Whatever Happened to Old Fashioned Love"

Answers begin on page 169.

129. What song did Merle Haggard write after seeing convicted murderer Jimmy "Rabbit" Hendricks take his last walk at San Quentin?

A) "Sing a Sad Song"
B) "The Fugitive"
C) "Branded Man"
D) "Sing Me Back Home"

130. The Dolly Parton/Sylvester Stallone movie *Rhinestone* was initially conceived as the film adaptation of what hit country song?

A) "Country Bumpkin"
B) "It's All Wrong, but It's All Right"
C) "Rhinestone Cowboy"
D) "Wasted Days and Wasted Nights"

131. What George Strait hit was co-written by Kerry Chater, the one-time bass player for Gary Puckett & the Union Gap?

A) "Does Fort Worth Ever Cross Your Mind?"
B) "Let's Fall to Pieces Together"
C) "Right or Wrong"
D) "You Look So Good in Love"

George Strait

132. What was the theme, sung by Johnny Lee, for the 1980 film *Urban Cowboy*?

A) "Could I Have This Dance"
B) "Lookin' for Love"
C) "Stand by Me"
D) "Love the World Away"

133. What record featured Jerry Reed impersonating Willie Nelson and George Jones?

A) "Gimme Back My Blues"
B) "Ko-Ko Joe"
C) "She Got the Goldmine (I Got the Shaft)"
D) "The Bird"

134. Which song provided Wynonna Judd with her name?

A) "I've Been Everywhere"
B) "Night Train"
C) "Route 66"
D) "Sweet Little Sixteen"

135. Which Beatles tune did Rosanne Cash take to the top of the country charts in 1989?

A) "Can't Buy Me Love"
B) "I Don't Want to Spoil the Party"
C) "I Feel Fine"
D) "I'll Cry Instead"

Answers begin on page 169.

136. **Which hit single came from Johnny Cash's *Johnny Cash at San Quentin* album?**
   A) "Folsom Prison Blues"
   B) "In the Jailhouse Now"
   C) "I Got Stripes"
   D) "A Boy Named Sue"

137. **Cuban-born bandleader Perez Prado, sometimes called "King of the Mambo," had one of his instrumental records reach the Top Twenty of the *Billboard* country charts in 1958. Which one was it?**
   A) "Cherry Pink and Apple Blossom White"
   B) "Patricia"
   C) "In a Little Spanish Town"
   D) "Mambo No. 5"

138. **In 1977, Loretta Lynn released *I Remember Patsy*, an album that paid tribute to her mentor, Patsy Cline. What single from the album topped the chart, giving Cline and Lynn a #1 hit with the same song?**
   A) "She's Got You"
   B) "Why Can't He Be You"
   C) "Sweet Dreams (of You)"
   D) "Crazy"

139. **What duet won Travis Tritt and Marty Stuart a 1992 Grammy?**
   A) "Honky Tonkin's What I Do Best"
   B) "Lord Have Mercy on the Working Man"
   C) "The Whiskey Ain't Workin'"
   D) "This One's Gonna Hurt You (For a Long, Long Time)"

140. **What Randy Travis record won its writers Song of the Year honors from the Academy of Country Music and the Country Music Association, as well as a Best Country Song Grammy?**
   A) "On the Other Hand"
   B) "Forever and Ever, Amen"
   C) "Hard Rock Bottom of Your Heart"
   D) "Point of Light"

141. **What song was a Top Ten hit for both Loretta Lynn and Emmylou Harris?**
   A) "Blue Kentucky Girl"
   B) "If I Could Only Win Your Love"
   C) "Success"
   D) "When the Tingle Becomes a Chill"

142. **Moe Bandy & Joe Stampley had several hit duets during the late 1970s and early 1980s. Which was the only one to go all the way to #1?**
   A) "Hey Joe (Hey Moe)"
   B) "Holding the Bag"
   C) "Just Good Ol' Boys"
   D) "Where's the Dress"

Answers begin on page 169.

143. **What 1958 pop and r&b hit for Little Willie John has been a Top Forty country hit twice, first for Freddy Fender in 1978, then for Mickey Gilley in 1982?**
   A) "Fever"
   B) "Talk to Me"
   C) "Heartbreak (It's Hurtin' Me)"
   D) "Sleep"

144. **What 1975 chart-topper contains the line, "Just because we are married don't mean we can't slip around"?**
   A) "Secret Love," Freddy Fender
   B) "Linda on My Mind," Conway Twitty
   C) "Always Wanting You," Merle Haggard
   D) "Blanket on the Ground," Billie Jo Spears

145. **What minor hit for Carl Smith in 1965 was the last of five #1 hits Charlie Rich had in 1974?**
   A) "There Won't Be Anymore"
   B) "I Don't See Me in Your Eyes Anymore"
   C) "I Love My Friend"
   D) "She Called Me Baby"

146. **What Ray Charles/Willie Nelson duet reached the #1 spot in 1985?**
   A) "It Ain't Gonna Worry My Mind"
   B) "Seven Spanish Angels"
   C) "Two Old Cats Like Us"
   D) "We Didn't See a Thing"

147. **What remake of a Webb Pierce hit gave Gail Davies her first Top Forty single, in 1978?**
   A) "No Love Have I"
   B) "Poison Love"
   C) "I'll Be There (If You Ever Want Me)"
   D) "I Don't Care"

148. **What song was a Top Twenty hit for Joe Sun in 1978, but a #1 record for Dolly Parton in 1980?**
   A) "Starting Over Again"
   B) "Old Flames (Can't Hold a Candle to You)"
   C) "You're the Only One"
   D) "9 to 5"

149. **What song was a hit for Ernest Tubb during World War II and for Merle Haggard during the Vietnam War?**
   A) "At Mail Call Today"
   B) "Deck of Cards"
   C) "Soldier's Last Letter"
   D) "There's a Star-Spangled Banner Waving Somewhere"

*Answers begin on page 169.

150. What song hit the Top Ten twice for George Jones, first on his own in 1966, then with Tammy Wynette in 1972?

A) "Color of the Blues"

B) "Take Me"

C) "Tender Years"

D) "A Picture of Me (without You)"

Brooks & Dunn

151. What Roger Miller waltz did Brooks & Dunn cover in 1998, taking it all the way to #1?

A) "King of the Road"

B) "One Dyin' and A-Buryin'"

C) "Husbands and Wives"

D) "The Last Word in Lonesome Is Me"

152. What song was a #1 hit for both Buck Owens and Emmylou Harris?

A) "Above and Beyond"

B) "Excuse Me (I Think I've Got a Heartache)"

C) "Love's Gonna Live Here"

D) "Together Again"

153. What was Glen Campbell's first #1 single?

A) "By the Time I Get to Phoenix"

B) "Gentle on My Mind"

C) "I Wanna Live"

D) "Dreams of the Everyday Housewife"

154. What was Mary Chapin Carpenter's first #1 hit?

A) "Down at the Twist and Shout"

B) "He Thinks He'll Keep Her"

C) "Passionate Kisses"

D) "Shut Up and Kiss Me"

155. What was the first John Denver record to top both the country and the pop charts?

A) "Annie's Song"

B) "Back Home Again"

C) "I'm Sorry"

D) "Thank God I'm a Country Boy"

156. Which of his hits did Dwight Yoakam write with Roger Miller?

A) "Turn It On, Turn It Up, Turn It Loose"

B) "I Got You"

C) "You're the One"

D) "It Only Hurts When I Cry"

157. Which of these Patsy Cline hits did not cross over to the pop Top Forty?

A) "Crazy"

B) "She's Got You"

C) "Sweet Dreams (of You)"

D) "Walkin' after Midnight"

Answers begin on page 169.

158. Which single spent more than a year in the Top Ten of the *Billboard* country charts?

A) "Bouquet of Roses," Eddy Arnold

B) "I'll Hold You in My Heart (till I Can Hold You in My Arms)," Eddy Arnold

C) "I'm Moving On," Hank Snow

D) "Lovesick Blues," Hank Williams

159. What was Gene Autry's theme song?

A) "Back in the Saddle Again"

B) "Cool Water"

C) "Don't Fence Me In"

D) "Mexicali Rose"

160. What song, written by disco queen Donna Summer and husband Bruce Sudano, gave Dolly Parton a #1 country hit in 1980?

A) "Sweet Summer Lovin'"

B) "Starting Over Again"

C) "Making Plans"

D) "Old Flames (Can't Hold a Candle to You)"

161. What was Bobby Bare's only #1 hit?

A) "Detroit City"   B) "Daddy What If?"   C) "Miller's Cave"   D) "Marie Laveau"

162. What Kenny Rogers song takes place "in a bar in Toledo across from the depot"?

A) "Coward of the County"

B) "The Gambler"

C) "Lucille"

D) "Share Your Love with Me"

163. George Morgan's first single went to the top of the country charts, a feat he never duplicated despite more than 30 charting singles. What was Morgan's sole #1?

A) "Almost"

B) "Candy Kisses"

C) "I Love Everything about You"

D) "Room Full of Roses"

164. Though she had 31 Top Forty singles, only Jean Shepard's first single went all the way to #1. What was it?

A) "Beautiful Lies"

B) "A Dear John Letter"

C) "A Satisfied Mind"

D) "Second Fiddle (to an Old Guitar)"

165. Johnny Cash took an interest in this song but agreed to let a newcomer named Henson Cargill have first crack at it. It ended up spending five weeks at #1 in 1968. What song was it?

A) "None of My Business"

B) "Row Row Row"

C) "Skip a Rope"

D) "A World of Our Own"

Answers begin on page 169.

166. What "instant folksong," penned by Danny Dill and Marijohn Wilkin, did Lefty Frizzell release in 1959?

A) "Forbidden Lovers"
B) "The Long Black Veil"
C) "Saginaw, Michigan"
D) "She's Gone, Gone, Gone"

167. On what Marty Robbins record did Grady Martin play a distorted six-string electric bass solo because of a malfunctioning pre-amp?

A) "Big Iron"   B) "Don't Worry"   C) "Devil Woman"   D) "Ruby Ann"

168. What Don Gibson song was inspired by reading a magazine interview with Bobby Darin?

A) "Oh Lonesome Me"
B) "I Can't Stop Loving You"
C) "Sea of Heartbreak"
D) "(I'd Be) a Legend in My Time"

169. What's the only George Hamilton IV single to reach the #1 spot on the *Billboard* country charts?

A) "Abilene"
B) "Break My Mind"
C) "Early Morning Rain"
D) "If You Don't Know I Ain't Gonna Tell You"

170. What was the first Tammy Wynette single to use strings?

A) "Apartment #9"
B) "I Don't Wanna Play House"
C) "Take Me to Your World"
D) "Stand by Your Man"

171. What 1969 Johnny Cash chart-topper did Carl Perkins write?

A) "Daddy Sang Bass"
B) "A Boy Named Sue"
C) "Blistered"
D) "Get Rhythm"

172. Sonny James had two #1 country hits with songs that had originally been pop hits for the Australian pop–folk group the Seekers. The first was "I'll Never Find Another You." What was the second?

A) "It's the Little Things"
B) "A World of Our Own"
C) "Born to Be with You"
D) "Georgy Girl"

173. What future Rodney Crowell #1 did Steve Wariner record for his *Life's Highway* album?

A) "I Couldn't Leave You If I Tried"
B) "She's Crazy for Leavin'"
C) "After All This Time"
D) "Above and Beyond"

*Answers begin on page 169.

174. **What was the first country version of a Beatles tune to hit #1?**
A) "I Don't Want to Spoil the Party"   C) "I'm Happy Just to Dance with You"
B) "I Feel Fine"   D) "Something"

175. **What song did Merle Haggard write about Dolly Parton after becoming infatuated with her while the two toured together?**
A) "Always Wanting You"   C) "Let's Chase Each Other around the Room"
B) "The Emptiest Arms in the World"   D) "You Take Me for Granted"

176. **What song has had the most versions placed on the *Billboard* country charts?**
A) "I Love You Because"   C) "Slipping Around"
B) "Making Believe"   D) "Sweet Dreams"

177. **Leon Payne hit #1 in 1950 with one of his songs but never had another record make the *Billboard* country charts. What was this one-hit wonder's big record?**
A) "I Love You Because"   C) "Psycho"
B) "Lost Highway"   D) "They'll Never Take Her Love from Me"

178. **What Loretta Lynn record did Decca accidentally release with the title "Here in Topeka"?**
A) "Fist City"   C) "Dear Uncle Sam"
B) "One's on the Way"   D) "Trouble in Paradise"

179. **What was Slim Willet's only charting hit, which went all the way to #1 in 1952?**
A) "Abilene Waltz"   C) "I'm a Tool-Pusher from Snyder"
B) "Don't Let the Stars Get in Your Eyes"   D) "Moon over Mexico"

180. **What was the B-side of Merle Haggard's single "The Legend of Bonnie & Clyde"?**
A) "Silver Wings"   C) "Good Times"
B) "Today I Started Loving You Again"   D) "You Don't Have Very Far to Go"

181. **What 1956 pop hit by the Chordettes did Sonny James remake for a #1 hit in 1968?**
A) "Born to Be with You"   C) "It's Just a Matter of Time"
B) "Since I Met You, Baby"   D) "Only Love Can Break a Heart"

182. **What was the first Roy Orbison record to make the country charts?**
A) "That Lovin' You Feelin' Again"   C) "Crying"
B) "In Dreams"   D) "You Got It"

*Answers begin on page 169.

183. **What was the first single written and/or produced by Billy Sherrill to top the *Billboard* country charts?**
    A) "Almost Persuaded," David Houston
    B) "Apartment #9," Tammy Wynette
    C) "Livin' in a House Full of Love," David Houston
    D) "Your Good Girl's Gonna Go Bad," Tammy Wynette

184. **What was Epic Records' first country hit?**
    A) "Cotton Mill Man," Jim & Jesse
    B) "Close All the Honky Tonks," Charlie Walker
    C) "Mountain of Love," David Houston
    D) "Apartment #9," Tammy Wynette

185. **What country standard, a hit in five different decades, begins, "Ev'rybody's goin' out and havin' fun/I'm just a fool for stayin' home and havin' none"?**
    A) "I'm a Fool to Love You"   C) "Oh Lonesome Me"
    B) "Flowers on the Wall"   D) "The Wild Side of Life"

186. **What Jack Greene hit was recorded only after Greene changed the title in order to sneak it past producer Owen Bradley, who had previously rejected it?**
    A) "There Goes My Everything"   C) "Until My Dreams Come True"
    B) "All the Time"   D) "Statue of a Fool"

187. **Sonny James's last #1 hit for Capitol was also the B-side of his first #1 hit, "Young Love." What was the song?**
    A) "Bright Lights, Big City"   C) "That's Why I Love You Like I Do"
    B) "Here Comes Honey Again"   D) "When the Snow Is on the Roses"

188. **What Hank Williams Jr. hit was co-written by noted film composer Lalo Schifrin?**
    A) "All for the Love of Sunshine"   C) "I'd Rather Be Gone"
    B) "Eleven Roses"   D) "I'll Think of Something"

189. **What 1972 #1 single was recorded for an episode of Rod Serling's TV show *Night Gallery*?**
    A) "Eleven Roses," Hank Williams Jr.
    B) "If You Leave Me Tonight I'll Cry," Jerry Wallace
    C) "She's Got to Be a Saint," Ray Price
    D) "That's Why I Love You Like I Do," Sonny James

Answers begin on page 169.

190. Which of Dave Dudley's hits was penned by Tom T. Hall?
A) "Six Days on the Road"
B) "Truck Drivin' Son-Of-A-Gun"
C) "George (and the North Woods)"
D) "The Pool Shark"

191. Which Tom T. Hall hit was written at the request of Stonewall Jackson?
A) "A Week in a County Jail"
B) "Ballad of Forty Dollars"
C) "I Like Beer"
D) "That Song Is Driving Me Crazy"

192. What song did Conway Twitty record in Russian to be played during the outer-space docking of the Apollo and Soyuz ships in 1975?
A) "Hello, Darlin'"
B) "I Can't Stop Loving You"
C) "I Can't See Me without You"
D) "You've Never Been This Far Before"

193. What Charley Pride chart-topper did Merle Haggard write?
A) "A Shoulder to Cry On"
B) "It's Gonna Take a Little Bit Longer"
C) "Don't Fight the Feelings of Love"
D) "She's Just an Old Love Turned Memory"

194. Beginning with their second single, the Judds had eight straight #1 hits. What was the duo's first single, which peaked at #17?
A) "Girls' Night Out"
B) "Had a Dream (for the Heart)"
C) "Mama He's Crazy"
D) "Love Is Alive"

195. The Davis Sisters had one #1 single, but no other records ever charted because one of the duo's members died two weeks before the single came out. What was that record?
A) "I Forgot More Than You'll Ever Know"
B) "Sorrow and Pain"
C) "Rock-A-Bye Boogie"
D) "You're Gone"

The Judds

196. What Merle Haggard song, written on behalf of Vietnam prisoners of war, reached #1 just five days after the first group of POW's left Hanoi?
A) "I Wonder If They Ever Think of Me"
B) "If We Make It through December"
C) "Soldier's Last Letter"
D) "Someday We'll Look Back"

*Answers begin on page 169.

197. What Waylon Jennings & Willie Nelson hit was inspired by an ad for r&b duo Ike & Tina Turner?

A) "Just to Satisfy You"
B) "Good Hearted Woman"
C) "I Can Get Off on You"
D) "Take It to the Limit"

198. What #1 country hit was written and performed by someone who would go on to become a story editor for the television drama *Magnum, P.I.*?

A) "It Couldn't Have Been Any Better," Johnny Duncan
B) "It Only Hurts for a Little While," Margo Smith
C) "Teddy Bear Song," Barbara Fairchild
D) "The White Knight," Cledus Maggard & the Citizen's Band

199. What hit did songwriter Gene Hood sue Conway Twitty over, claiming that it infringed on "Too Much of You," a single Hood had written for Lynn Anderson?

A) "Linda on My Mind"
B) "Touch the Hand"
C) "How Much More Can She Stand?"
D) "I've Never Seen the Likes of You"

200. What Merle Haggard hit was penned by Dolly Parton?

A) "Always Wanting You"
B) "Kentucky Gambler"
C) "Old Man from the Mountain"
D) "It's All in the Movies"

201. What song begins with the line, "Don't look so sad; I know it's over"?

A) "Empty Arms"
B) "For the Good Times"
C) "Help Me Make It through the Night"
D) "I Won't Mention It Again"

202. What David Allan Coe song was originally titled "Tell Me Lady, Can You Pray"?

A) "Mona Lisa Lost Her Smile"
B) "Would You Be My Lady"
C) "Take This Job and Shove It"
D) "Would You Lay with Me (in a Field of Stone)"

203. What single gave Billy Ray Cyrus a pop crossover smash in 1992?

A) "Achy Breaky Heart"
B) "Friends in Low Places"
C) "She's Not Cryin' Anymore"
D) "Some Gave All"

204. What Lefty Frizzell song was a #1 hit for both Johnny Rodriguez and Merle Haggard?

A) "The Long Black Veil"
B) "Saginaw, Michigan"
C) "That's the Way Love Goes"
D) "Life's Like Poetry"

Answers begin on page 169.

205. What song was Waylon Jennings set to perform on the *1974 Country Music Association Awards Show* when he was told he would have to shorten it, prompting him to walk off the set?

A) "Are You Sure Hank Done It This Way?"
B) "Good Hearted Woman"
C) "I'm a Ramblin' Man"
D) "Luckenbach, Texas (Back to the Basics of Love)"

206. What 1950s classic begins with the line, "Now blue ain't the word for the way that I feel"?

A) "Crazy Arms"
B) "I Don't Hurt Anymore"
C) "I'm Moving On"
D) "The Wild Side of Life"

207. What western classic starts with the line, "The cattle are prowlin' and the coyotes are howlin' way out where the dogies bawl"?

A) "Back in the Saddle Again"
B) "Cattle Call"
C) "Cool Water"
D) "Don't Fence Me In"

208. What David Kersh hit did Brad Paisley write before starting his own recording career?

A) "Goodnight Sweetheart"
B) "Another You"
C) "Day In, Day Out"
D) "If I Never Stop Loving You"

209. What song did Blake Shelton record before Toby Keith, only to leave it off his album when his label decided it wouldn't be suitable for a new artist?

A) "How Do You Like Me Now?!"
B) "I Wanna Talk about Me"
C) "I'm Just Talkin' about Tonight"
D) "Who's Your Daddy?"

210. What was Conway Twitty's first country hit?

A) "Guess My Eyes Were Bigger Than My Heart"
B) "Hello Darlin'"
C) "It's Only Make Believe"
D) "You've Never Been This Far Before"

211. Which Tim McGraw hit was penned by Phil Vassar?

A) "My Next Thirty Years"
B) "Some Things Don't Change"
C) "Grown Men Don't Cry"
D) "Angry All the Time"

212. To whose place would you go if you wanted a "slaw burger, fries, and a bottle of Ski"?

A) "Marty Gray" B) "Dumas Walker" C) "Juanita Jones" D) "Cornell Crawford"

Answers begin on page 169.

213. In what song did Billy Bob tell the town he loved Charlene by painting the local water tower?

A) "Bluer Than Blue"   B) "Something in Red"   C) "John Deere Green"   D) "Brown to Blue"

214. What honky-tonk classic does Vern Gosdin reference in his 1988 hit "Set 'Em Up Joe"?

A) "Dim Lights, Thick Smoke (and Loud, Loud Music)"
B) "On Tap, in the Can, or in the Bottle"
C) "Walking the Floor over You"
D) "Your Cheatin' Heart"

Dolly Parton

215. What was Dolly Parton's first #1 record?

A) "Dumb Blonde"
B) "Joshua"
C) "Coat of Many Colors"
D) "Jolene"

216. Lloyd Maines, the father of Dixie Chicks vocalist Natalie Maines, played in a group called the Maines Brothers Band that had one Top Forty country hit. What was it?

A) "Louisiana Anna"
B) "Some of Shelly's Blues"
C) "Everybody Needs Love on Saturday Night"
D) "When My Blue Moon Turns to Gold Again"

217. What Holly Dunn record drew criticism from the National Organization for Women and wound up being the last single of her career to crack even the Top Fifty?

A) "Daddy's Hands"
B) "You Really Had Me Going"
C) "Heart Full of Love"
D) "Maybe I Mean Yes"

218. In which of these songs does a mother turn her daughter out into the streets as a prostitute?

A) "Amanda"   B) "Bobbie Sue"   C) "Darlene"   D) "Fancy"

219. Which of his hits did Rodney Crowell write with Roy Orbison?

A) "Victim or a Fool"
B) "When I'm Free Again"
C) "Now That We're Alone"
D) "What Kind of Love"

Answers begin on page 169.

220. In what song does Jessica Andrews sing about being "Rosemary's granddaughter"?

A) "I Will Be There for You"   C) "Who I Am"

B) "You Go First (Do You Wanna Kiss)"   D) "There's More to Me Than You"

221. In what song does Montgomery Gentry "work all day in the muck and the mire"?

A) "Daddy Won't Sell the Farm"   C) "My Town"

B) "Hillbilly Shoes"   D) "Self-Made Man"

222. In which of her hits does Mary Chapin Carpenter buy "a pack of Camels, a burrito, and a Barq's"?

A) "Down at the Twist and Shout"   C) "Quittin' Time"

B) "I Feel Lucky"   D) "Shut Up and Kiss Me"

223. Which hit did Keith Urban write with two members of the Go-Gos rock group?

A) "But for the Grace of God"   C) "Somebody Like You"

B) "Where the Blacktop Ends"   D) "Raining on Sunday"

224. What Mary Chapin Carpenter hit took its title from an old slogan for Geritol multivitamins?

A) "Never Had It So Good"   C) "He Thinks He'll Keep Her"

B) "Not Too Much to Ask"   D) "Tender When I Want to Be"

225. What Shania Twain video did Sean Penn direct?

A) "Dance with the One That Brought You"   C) "Whose Bed Have Your Boots Been Under?"

B) "Any Man of Mine"   D) "You Win My Love"

226. What Ronnie Milsap hit was written as the result of a Bible study?

A) "(I'm a) Stand by My Woman Man"   C) "What a Difference You've Made in My Life"

B) "Let My Love Be Your Pillow"   D) "She Keeps the Home Fires Burning"

227. What Conway Twitty hit was written as a tribute to the Grand Ole Opry?

A) "Play, Guitar, Play"   C) "Boogie Grass Band"

B) "The Grandest Lady of Them All"   D) "Saturday Night Special"

228. Which Johnny Paycheck hit was written by David Allan Coe?

A) "11 Months and 29 Days"   C) "I'm the Only Hell (Mama Ever Raised)"

B) "Colorado Kool-Aid"   D) "Take This Job and Shove It"

*Answers begin on page 169.

229. What Travis Tritt video reunited the members of the Eagles for the first time in 14 years?
A) "Anymore"
B) "Here's a Quarter (Call Someone Who Cares)"
C) "Take It Easy"
D) "Foolish Pride"

230. Which of these Brenda Lee singles made the Top Five of the country charts?
A) "Big Four Poster Bed"
B) "Break It to Me Gently"
C) "Fool #1"
D) "I'm Sorry"

231. Ronnie Milsap's acceptance speech for his Entertainer of the Year award at the *1977 Country Music Association Awards Show* inspired songwriters John Bettis and R.C. Bannon to write what song that would later become a hit for Milsap?
A) "Let's Take the Long Way around the World"
B) "Nobody Likes Sad Songs"
C) "In No Time at All"
D) "Only One Love in My Life"

232. What song did writer Don Schlitz have a minor chart hit with, before Kenny Rogers recorded it and made it an award-winning country and pop smash?
A) "Lucille"
B) "The Gambler"
C) "You Decorated My Life"
D) "She Believes in Me"

233. With which Clint Eastwood movie theme did Eddie Rabbitt score a #1 country hit?
A) "Every Which Way but Loose"
B) "Any Which Way You Can"
C) "Honky Tonk Man"
D) "The Good, the Bad, and the Ugly"

234. Which recording from the *Urban Cowboy* soundtrack was the first to top the country charts?
A) "The Devil Went Down to Georgia," The Charlie Daniels Band
B) "Stand by Me," Mickey Gilley
C) "Lookin' for Love," Johnny Lee
D) "Could I Have This Dance," Anne Murray

235. Which of these hits gave Barbara Mandrell's stage band its name?
A) "Do Right Woman—Do Right Man"
B) "The Midnight Oil"
C) "Standing Room Only"
D) "Crackers"

*Answers begin on page 169.

236. Merle Haggard's backing band took its name from which of these hits?
A) "Branded Man"
B) "The Fugitive"
C) "(My Friends Are Gonna Be) Strangers"
D) "Swinging Doors"

237. What was the first #1 country hit recorded in England?
A) "I Got Mexico," Eddy Raven
B) "You're My Jamaica," Charley Pride
C) "Hello Vietnam," Johnnie Wright
D) "England Swings," Roger Miller

238. What was the first cover of a Hank Williams song to reach #1 on the country charts?
A) "I Can't Help It (If I'm Still in Love with You)," Linda Ronstadt
B) "Honky Tonk Blues," Charley Pride
C) "Honky Tonkin'," Hank Williams Jr.
D) "Kaw-Liga," Ronnie Milsap

239. Which of Jo Dee Messina's hits had previously been a #1 single for Dottie West?
A) "Bye-Bye"   B) "That's the Way"   C) "Lesson in Leavin'"   D) "Was That My Life?"

240. Which of these Merle Haggard hits was a duet with actor Clint Eastwood?
A) "Bar Room Buddies"
B) "The Bull and the Beaver"
C) "I Can't Hold Myself in Line"
D) "C.C. Waterback"

241. Which Anne Murray hit was originally intended to be a duet between her and Kenny Rogers?
A) "You Needed Me"
B) "Could I Have This Dance"
C) "I Just Fall in Love Again"
D) "Blessed Are the Believers"

242. Which George Jones & Tammy Wynette hit begins "in a pawn shop in Chicago"?
A) "(We're Not) the Jet Set"
B) "The Ceremony"
C) "Golden Ring"
D) "Near You"

243. Which Statler Brothers record is featured in the film *Pulp Fiction*?
A) "Flowers on the Wall"
B) "Bed of Roses"
C) "You'll Be Back (Every Night in My Dreams)"
D) "I'll Go to My Grave Loving You"

244. Which Kenny Rogers & Dottie West duet was released under only West's name?
A) "Anyone Who Isn't Me Tonight"
B) "All I Ever Need Is You"
C) "'Til I Can Make It on My Own"
D) "What Are We Doin' in Love?"

Answers begin on page 169.

245. In which song are the Statler Brothers "smoking cigarettes and watching Captain Kangaroo"?

A) "Do You Remember These"
C) "A Child of the Fifties"
B) "Flowers on the Wall"
D) "Whatever Happened to Randolph Scott?"

246. Which of Alan Jackson's singles had originally been a hit for Charly McClain?

A) "I'll Try"
B) "Song for the Life"
C) "Home"
D) "Who's Cheatin' Who"

247. Which Eddie Rabbitt hit was used in a Miller Beer commercial?

A) "Drivin' My Life Away"
C) "I Love a Rainy Night"
B) "Drinkin' My Baby (off My Mind)"
D) "I Can't Help Myself"

248. What song by 1950s rocker Little Richard was a #1 hit for Waylon Jennings in 1983?

A) "Jenny, Jenny"
B) "Lucille"
C) "Rip It Up"
D) "Ooh! My Soul"

249. Sammy Johns, who wrote John Conlee's #1 1983 hit "Common Man," had one Top Five pop hit in 1975 with a song later covered by Sammy Kershaw. What was that song?

A) "Chevy Van"
C) "Third-Rate Romance"
B) "Early Morning Love"
D) "Undercover Angel"

250. Which Little Jimmy Dickens hit provided the name for his backing band?

A) "Take an Old Cold 'Tater (and Wait)"
B) "Country Boy"
C) "May the Bird of Paradise Fly up Your Nose"
D) "(You've Been Quite a Doll) Raggedy Ann"

251. Which Clay Walker hit did Lonestar's Richie McDonald co-write?

A) "Only on Days That End in 'Y'"
C) "Then What"
B) "She's Always Right"
D) "You're Beginning to Get to Me"

252. Which of Deana Carter's first four singles didn't hit #1?

A) "Strawberry Wine"
C) "Count Me In"
B) "We Danced Anyway"
D) "How Do I Get There?"

253. What Ricky Skaggs video featured Bill Monroe in New York's Times Square?

A) "Country Boy"
C) "Highway 40 Blues"
B) "Don't Get above Your Raising"
D) "Uncle Pen"

Answers begin on page 169.

254. What John Anderson hit was co-written by award-winning director Robert Altman?

A) "Black Sheep"

B) "Goin' Down Hill"

C) "She Sure Got Away with My Heart"

D) "Would You Catch a Falling Star?"

255. What Statler Brothers hit was inspired by a viewing of the film *Giant*?

A) "The Class of '57"

B) "Do You Remember These"

C) "Elizabeth"

D) "The Movies"

256. What song did Bill Anderson write as the result of bumping into an ex-girlfriend who had married the weatherman at an Atlanta TV station where Anderson was about to be interviewed?

A) "Always Remember"

B) "I Love You Drops"

C) "Don't She Look Good?"

D) "Still"

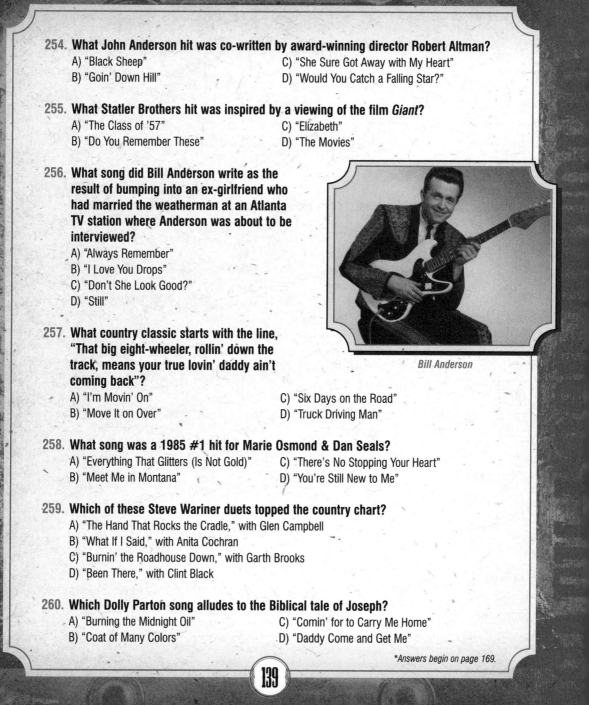

Bill Anderson

257. What country classic starts with the line, "That big eight-wheeler, rollin' down the track, means your true lovin' daddy ain't coming back"?

A) "I'm Movin' On"

B) "Move It on Over"

C) "Six Days on the Road"

D) "Truck Driving Man"

258. What song was a 1985 #1 hit for Marie Osmond & Dan Seals?

A) "Everything That Glitters (Is Not Gold)"

B) "Meet Me in Montana"

C) "There's No Stopping Your Heart"

D) "You're Still New to Me"

259. Which of these Steve Wariner duets topped the country chart?

A) "The Hand That Rocks the Cradle," with Glen Campbell

B) "What If I Said," with Anita Cochran

C) "Burnin' the Roadhouse Down," with Garth Brooks

D) "Been There," with Clint Black

260. Which Dolly Parton song alludes to the Biblical tale of Joseph?

A) "Burning the Midnight Oil"

B) "Coat of Many Colors"

C) "Comin' for to Carry Me Home"

D) "Daddy Come and Get Me"

*Answers begin on page 169.

261. Which John Anderson hit featured guest vocals by Waylon Jennings?
A) "I'm Just an Old Chunk of Coal (but I'm Gonna Be a Diamond Someday)"
B) "Somewhere between Ragged and Right"
C) "Country 'til I Die"
D) "Honky Tonk Crowd"

262. Which Alabama hit featured guest vocals by K.T. Oslin?
A) "You've Got the Touch"
B) "Face to Face"
C) "Fallin' Again"
D) "If I Had You"

263. What Aerosmith pop hit did Mark Chesnutt turn into a country chart-topper?
A) "Cryin'"
B) "Dream On"
C) "Fever"
D) "I Don't Want to Miss a Thing"

264. Shania Twain's 1993 debut album, *Shania Twain*, featured only one song that she had written. Which one was it?
A) "What Made You Say That?"
B) "Dance with the One That Brought You"
C) "God Ain't Gonna Getcha for That"
D) "Forget Me"

265. What song was a #1 duet for Charly McClain and Mickey Gilley?
A) "Candy Man"
B) "I Hate the Way I Love It"
C) "Paradise Tonight"
D) "The Right Stuff"

266. In which song did Mel Tillis grant Webb Pierce a half-interest in exchange for a pair of boots?
A) "Honky Tonk Song"
B) "How Come Your Dog Won't Bite Nobody but Me?"
C) "I Ain't Never"
D) "I'm Tired"

267. What Steve Azar video features Academy Award-nominated actor Morgan Freeman?
A) "I Don't Have to Be Me ('til Monday)"
B) "Someday"
C) "I Never Stopped Lovin' You"
D) "Waitin' on Joe"

268. Which song from his 1999 *Everywhere We Go* album does Kenny Chesney sing as a duet with Randy Travis?
A) "Baptism"
B) "California"
C) "I Might Get over You"
D) "Life Is Good"

*Answers begin on page 169.

269. Which of these tracks from the *O Brother, Where Art Thou*? soundtrack actually was recorded in the 1920s?

A) "Big Rock Candy Mountain," Harry McClintock
B) "Hard Time Killing Floor Blues," Chris Thomas King
C) "I Am a Man of Constant Sorrow," The Soggy Bottom Boys
D) "In the Highways," The Peasall Sisters

270. Which of these songs was Ernest Ashworth's only #1 hit?

A) "Each Moment (Spent with You)"
B) "Everybody but Me"
C) "I Take the Chance"
D) "Talk Back Trembling Lips"

271. To which Toby Keith record does Jessica Andrews allude in her 2003 hit "There's More to Me Than You"?

A) "Courtesy of the Red, White & Blue (The Angry American)"
B) "How Do You Like Me Now?!"
C) "I Wanna Talk about Me"
D) "You Shouldn't Kiss Me Like This"

272. What song was a Top Forty hit for Sawyer Brown, Steve Earle, and Dave Dudley?

A) "Hillbilly Highway"
B) "Nowhere Road"
C) "Keep on Truckin'"
D) "Six Days on the Road"

273. What's the first track on the Dixie Chicks' *Fly* album?

A) "Hello Mr. Heartache"
B) "Cowboy Take Me Away"
C) "If I Fall You're Going Down with Me"
D) "Ready to Run"

274. Which Gary Allan video featured an actress he ended up marrying?

A) "Her Man"
B) "It Would Be You"
C) "I'll Take Today"
D) "Smoke Rings in the Dark"

275. What 1956 Johnny Horton record did Dwight Yoakam remake for his first hit?

A) "All Grown Up"
B) "Honky-Tonk Man"
C) "I'm A One-Woman Man"
D) "The Woman I Need"

276. What was Steve Wariner's very first single, which he re-recorded and took to #3 in 1999?

A) "Every Little Whisper"
B) "Two Teardrops"
C) "I'm Already Taken"
D) "Been There"

*Answers begin on page 169.

277. What video won the first CMT Flameworthy Video of the Year award?
A) "Modern-Day Bonnie and Clyde," Travis Tritt
B) "Only in America," Brooks & Dunn
C) "I Wanna Talk about Me," Toby Keith
D) "Young," Kenny Chesney

278. What was Barbara Fairchild's only #1 record?
A) "Baby Doll"   B) "Kid Stuff"   C) "Little Girl Feeling"   D) "Teddy Bear Song"

279. What Alan Jackson song was inspired by a General Electric radio his father won in a raffle?
A) "Chasin' That Neon Rainbow"
B) "Drive (for Daddy Gene)"
C) "Little Man"
D) "Where I Come From"

280. What's the first track on the American version of Shania Twain's *Come on Over* album?
A) "Man! I Feel Like a Woman!"
B) "Love Gets Me Every Time"
C) "I'm Holdin' on to Love (to Save My Life)"
D) "Come on Over"

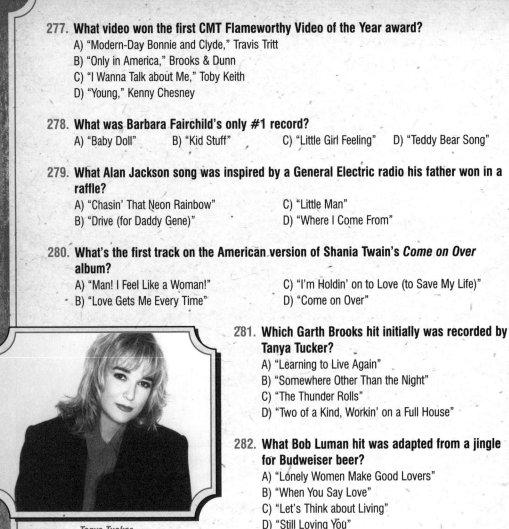

Tanya Tucker

281. Which Garth Brooks hit initially was recorded by Tanya Tucker?
A) "Learning to Live Again"
B) "Somewhere Other Than the Night"
C) "The Thunder Rolls"
D) "Two of a Kind, Workin' on a Full House"

282. What Bob Luman hit was adapted from a jingle for Budweiser beer?
A) "Lonely Women Make Good Lovers"
B) "When You Say Love"
C) "Let's Think about Living"
D) "Still Loving You"

283. What Phil Vassar song was inspired by a documentary on supermodel Cindy Crawford?
A) "Carlene"
B) "Just Another Day in Paradise"
C) "Right on the Money"
D) "Rose Bouquet"

*Answers begin on page 169.

284. **What was the first Steve Wariner single on which he played his own guitar solo?**
A) "I'm Already Taken"
B) "All Roads Lead to You"
C) "Midnight Fire"
D) "Some Fools Never Learn"

285. **What was the first Wynonna Judd single that didn't top the *Billboard* country chart?**
A) "She Is His Only Need"
B) "I Saw the Light"
C) "No One Else on Earth"
D) "My Strongest Weakness"

286. **What 1950s doo-wop classic is incorporated into the Ronnie Milsap hit "Lost in the Fifties Tonight"?**
A) "Goodnite Sweetheart, Goodnite," The Spaniels
B) "In the Still of the Night," The Five Satins
C) "Oh What a Nite," The Dells
D) "Tonite, Tonite," The Mello-Kings

287. **On what chart-topping 1987 hit did Kenny Rogers and Ronnie Milsap collaborate?**
A) "Where Do the Nights Go"
B) "Make No Mistake, She's Mine"
C) "Old Folks"
D) "Tomb of the Unknown Love"

288. **What was Dolly Parton's first record?**
A) "Dumb Blonde"   B) "Jolene"   C) "Puppy Love"   D) "The Love You Gave"

289. **Which Alabama hit did Vince Gill co-write?**
A) "Here We Are"
B) "I'm in a Hurry (and Don't Know Why)"
C) "Reckless"
D) "Then Again"

290. **What Kenny Chesney hit grew out of a line that songwriters Mark Alan Springer and Shaye Smith dropped from the Collin Raye hit "One Boy, One Girl"?**
A) "Fall in Love"   B) "She's Got It All"   C) "Me and You"   D) "That's Why I'm Here"

291. **What's the first track on Garth Brooks's *Ropin' the Wind* album?**
A) "Against the Grain"
B) "Burning Bridges"
C) "Rodeo"
D) "What She's Doing Now"

292. **Which of the Oak Ridge Boys' hits was a cover of a song previously recorded by the r&b–gospel act the Staple Singers?**
A) "Dream On"
B) "Sail Away"
C) "It Takes a Little Rain (to Make Love Grow)"
D) "Touch a Hand, Make a Friend"

Answers begin on page 169.

293. Which of Glen Campbell's hits did Neil Diamond write?
A) "Hound Dog Man"   C) "See You on Sunday"
B) "Can You Fool"   D) "Sunflower"

294. What song, inspired by a loss at the Grammys, ultimately won a Grammy for Rosanne Cash?
A) "Ain't No Money"
B) "I Don't Know Why You Don't Want Me"
C) "Seven Year Ache"
D) "If You Change Your Mind"

295. What was Wynonna Judd's first solo single?
A) "I Saw the Light"   C) "She Is His Only Need"
B) "One Hundred and Two"   D) "No One Else on Earth"

296. What Trisha Yearwood hit features a couple named Katy and Tommy?
A) "A Perfect Love"   C) "She's in Love with the Boy"
B) "Powerful Thing"   D) "Wrong Side of Memphis"

297. What's the first track on Billy Ray Cyrus's *Some Gave All* album?
A) "Achy Breaky Heart"   C) "She's Not Crying Anymore"
B) "Could've Been Me"   D) "Some Gave All"

298. What song was a #3 hit for one-time Garth Brooks guitarist Ty England in 1995?
A) "Irresistible You"   C) "Should've Asked Her Faster"
B) "Redneck Son"   D) "Smoke in Her Eyes"

299. Which Dixie Chicks song was the subject of a $500,000 lawsuit by the publishers of the gospel standard "I'll Fly Away" against Sony Entertainment?
A) "Goodbye Earl"   B) "Fly"   C) "Sin Wagon"   D) "There's Your Trouble"

300. What Travis Tritt video featured actor Billy Bob Thornton as the lead character?
A) "It's a Great Day to Be Alive"   C) "Strong Enough to Be Your Man"
B) "Modern Day Bonnie and Clyde"   D) "Love of a Woman"

301. With what song did Clint Black and Martina McBride have a hit in 1997?
A) "A Bad Goodbye"   C) "Something That We Do"
B) "Still Holding On"   D) "When I Said I Do"

Answers begin on page 169.

302. What Elton John song did Tim McGraw cover on his 2002 *Tim McGraw & the Dancehall Doctors* album?

A) "Daniel"

B) "Levon"

C) "Sorry Seems to Be the Hardest Word"

D) "Tiny Dancer"

303. What 1957 pop hit for the Tune Weavers did Ronnie Milsap take to the top of the country charts in 1986?

A) "Happy, Happy Birthday Baby"

B) "In the Still of the Nite"

C) "Snap Your Fingers"

D) "Any Day Now"

304. What's the only song to reach #1 twice for the same artist?

A) "Coal Miner's Daughter," Loretta Lynn

B) "I Will Always Love You," Dolly Parton

C) "Sweet Dreams (of You)," Patsy Cline

D) "Walking the Floor over You," Ernest Tubb

305. What was Jack Blanchard & Misty Morgan's only #1 hit?

A) "Humphrey the Camel"

B) "Somewhere in Virginia in the Rain"

C) "Tennessee Bird Walk"

D) "You've Got Your Troubles (I've Got Mine)"

306. What song did writers Dickey Lee, Tommy Rocco, and Johnny Russell unsuccessfully pitch to George Jones, only to have George Strait take it to the top of the charts?

A) "The Chair"

B) "The Fireman"

C) "Does Fort Worth Ever Cross Your Mind"

D) "Let's Fall to Pieces Together"

307. On which of her singles did Janie Fricke begin spelling her name "Frickie"?

A) "He's a Heartache (Looking for a Place to Happen)"

B) "Tell Me a Lie"

C) "The First Word in Memory Is Me"

D) "Always Have Always Will"

308. What song spent 10 weeks at #1 in 1959 for the family trio The Browns?

A) "Would You Care?"

B) "Beyond the Shadow"

C) "The Three Bells"

D) "Scarlet Ribbons (for Her Hair)"

309. What song did Johnny Cash record with rock band U2 for their *Zooropa* album?

A) "Daddy's Going to Pay for Your Crashed Car"

B) "Some Days Are Better Than Others"

C) "The Wanderer"

D) "Slow Dancing"

*Answers begin on page 169.

310. What's the first track on Garth Brooks's *No Fences* album?
A) "Friends in Low Places"
B) "New Way to Fly"
C) "The Thunder Rolls"
D) "Two of a Kind, Workin' on a Full House"

311. Which Faith Hill hit was used in the film *Pearl Harbor*?
A) "The Way You Love Me"
B) "There Will Come a Day"
C) "There You'll Be"
D) "If My Heart Had Wings"

312. What's the first track on the Dixie Chicks' *Wide Open Spaces* album?
A) "I Can Love You Better"
B) "Let 'Er Rip"
C) "There's Your Trouble"
D) "Wide Open Spaces"

313. Which of pop vocal group *NSYNC's hits did Alabama remake with the group in 1999?
A) "It's Gonna Be Me"
B) "God Must Have Spent a Little More Time on You"
C) "This I Promise You"
D) "Tearin' Up My Heart"

314. What song was a #1 hit for Earl Thomas Conley and Emmylou Harris?
A) "All Tangled Up in Love"
B) "I Believe in You"
C) "Too Many Times"
D) "We Believe in Happy Endings"

315. What Ricky Skaggs hit features a quote from the "Looney Tunes Theme" in one of its solos?
A) "Country Boy"
B) "Heartbroke"
C) "Uncle Pen"
D) "Honey (Open That Door)"

316. What Supremes pop hit did Bill Anderson and Jan Howard turn into a Top Five country record?
A) "My World Is Empty without You"
B) "Someday We'll Be Together"
C) "Where Did Our Love Go?"
D) "You Can't Hurry Love"

317. What's the first track on Shania Twain's *The Woman in Me* album?
A) "Any Man of Mine"
B) "Home Ain't Where the Heart Is (Anymore)"
C) "Whose Bed Have Your Boots Been Under?"
D) "If You're Not in It for Love (I'm Outta Here)"

Answers begin on page 169.

318. **What's the theme song for the television show *Austin City Limits*?**
    A) "Black Rose," Billy Joe Shaver   C) "Whiskey River," Willie Nelson
    B) "London Homesick Blues," Gary P. Nunn   D) "Tecumseh Valley," Townes Van Zandt

319. **What Johnny Cash classic begins, "I keep a close watch on this heart of mine"?**
    A) "Cry! Cry! Cry!"
    B) "Guess Things Happen That Way"
    C) "I Walk the Line"
    D) "Ring of Fire"

320. **What record, sung by Bobby Bare, was erroneously credited to his friend Bill Parsons?**
    A) "The All-American Boy"
    B) "Shame on Me"
    C) "Detroit City"
    D) "500 Miles Away from Home"

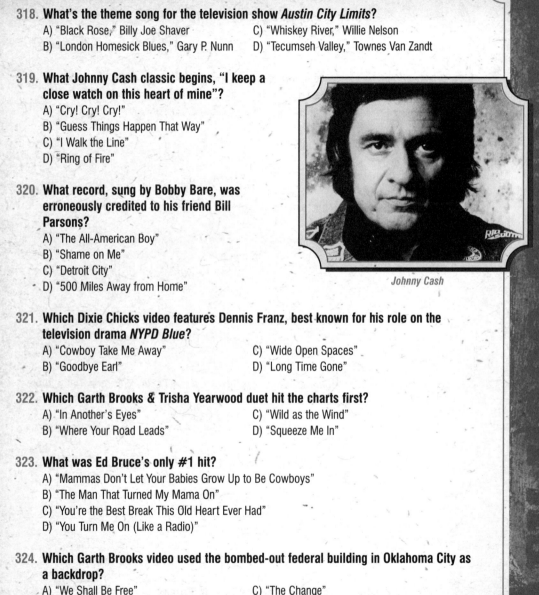

Johnny Cash

321. **Which Dixie Chicks video features Dennis Franz, best known for his role on the television drama *NYPD Blue*?**
    A) "Cowboy Take Me Away"   C) "Wide Open Spaces"
    B) "Goodbye Earl"   D) "Long Time Gone"

322. **Which Garth Brooks & Trisha Yearwood duet hit the charts first?**
    A) "In Another's Eyes"   C) "Wild as the Wind"
    B) "Where Your Road Leads"   D) "Squeeze Me In"

323. **What was Ed Bruce's only #1 hit?**
    A) "Mammas Don't Let Your Babies Grow Up to Be Cowboys"
    B) "The Man That Turned My Mama On"
    C) "You're the Best Break This Old Heart Ever Had"
    D) "You Turn Me On (Like a Radio)"

324. **Which Garth Brooks video used the bombed-out federal building in Oklahoma City as a backdrop?**
    A) "We Shall Be Free"   C) "The Change"
    B) "The River"   D) "Standing outside the Fire"

Answers begin on page 169.

325. **What was Shelly West's only #1 hit as a solo act?**
A) "Another Honky-Tonk Night on Broadway"   C) "I Just Came Here to Dance"
B) "Flight 309 to Tennessee"   D) "José Cuervo"

326. **What was the last Hank Williams record to enter the charts before his death?**
A) "I Won't Be Home No More"   C) "Lost Highway"
B) "I'll Never Get out of This World Alive"   D) "Your Cheatin' Heart"

327. **What was Gene Watson's only #1 hit?**
A) "Fourteen Carat Mind"
B) "Love in the Hot Afternoon"
C) "Paper Rosie"
D) "You're Out Doing What I'm Here Doing Without"

328. **Which Garth Brooks video featured cameos from Whoopi Goldberg, Gen. Colin Powell, Elizabeth Taylor, Jay Leno, and others?**
A) "The Dance"   C) "If Tomorrow Never Comes"
B) "We Shall Be Free"   D) "The Change"

329. **What Diamond Rio video featured Martin Sheen as a crazed evangelist?**
A) "Bubba Hyde"   C) "Mama, Don't Forget to Pray for Me"
B) "It's All in Your Head"   D) "Nowhere Bound"

330. **What Joe Diffie video featured cameo appearances by Porter Wagoner, Little Jimmy Dickens, and r&b singer Sam Moore?**
A) "Prop Me Up beside the Jukebox (If I Die)"   C) "Pickup Man"
B) "C-O-U-N-T-R-Y"   D) "This Is Your Brain"

331. **In what guest-filled Vince Gill video does Reba McEntire appear as a waitress?**
A) "Don't Let Our Love Start Slippin' Away"   C) "What the Cowgirls Do"
B) "One More Last Chance"   D) "The Heart Won't Lie"

332. **What was the first of Merle Haggard's hits that he wrote?**
A) "Sing a Sad Song"   C) "(My Friends Are Gonna Be) Strangers"
B) "Just Between the Two of Us"   D) "I'm Gonna Break Every Heart I Can"

333. **Which of Alan Jackson's hits was written by Tom T. Hall?**
A) "Little Bitty"   B) "Little Man"   C) "Tall, Tall Trees"   D) "Where I Come From"

Answers begin on page 169.

334. In what video did pop singer Huey Lewis play Reba McEntire's husband?
A) "For My Broken Heart"
B) "Is There Life Out There"
C) "I Know How He Feels"
D) "What Am I Gonna Do About You?"

335. Kris Kristofferson plays Lorrie Morgan's love interest in which video?
A) "I Guess You Had to Be There"
B) "Something in Red"
C) "Watch Me"
D) "We Both Walk"

336. What K.T. Oslin video spoofed Frankenstein movies?
A) "80's Ladies"
B) "Come Next Monday"
C) "Do Ya"
D) "Hold Me"

337. Which Dolly Parton video featured Billy Ray Cyrus, Mary Chapin Carpenter, Kathy Mattea, and Tanya Tucker?
A) "More Where That Came From"
B) "Runaway Feelin'"
C) "Romeo"
D) "Why'd You Come in Here Lookin' Like That"

338. Which BlackHawk video was filmed at the home of renowned Georgia folk artist Howard Finster?
A) "Every Once in a While"
B) "I Sure Can Smell the Rain"
C) "That's Just about Right"
D) "Almost a Memory Now"

339. What was the only #1 *Billboard* hit for Little Texas?
A) "What Might Have Been"
B) "Amy's Back in Austin"
C) "My Love"
D) "God Blessed Texas"

340. In what Aaron Tippin video did Reba McEntire play an exasperated bar manager?
A) "Honky-Tonk Superman"
B) "I Wouldn't Have It Any Other Way"
C) "My Blue Angel"
D) "She Feels Like a Brand New Man Tonight"

341. Which of these was never a country hit for Conway Twitty?
A) "Heartache Tonight"
B) "Hello Darlin'"
C) "I Can't Stop Loving You"
D) "It's Only Make Believe"

342. Which of these songs was a Faith Hill hit?
A) "Breathe"
B) "Every Breath You Take"
C) "I Breathe In, I Breathe Out"
D) "The Air That I Breathe"

*Answers begin on page 169.

343. Which song was a hit for Steve Wariner?
A) "Heaven in My Woman's Eyes"
B) "Heaven Only Knows"
C) "Holes in the Floor of Heaven"
D) "I May Never Get to Heaven"

344. Which of these hits did Randy Travis sing?
A) "Forever and Ever, Amen"
B) "Forever Love"
C) "Forever's as Far As I'll Go"
D) "Forever Again"

345. Which song topped the charts for George Strait?
A) "Fool for Your Love"
B) "Fool Hearted Memory"
C) "(Now and Then, There's) A Fool Such As I"
D) "The Fool"

346. All four of these songs reached the country charts twice for the same artist, but only one of them was the same recording both times. Which one?
A) "The Tin Man," Kenny Chesney
B) "Big River," Johnny Cash
C) "Sweet Dreams," Don Gibson
D) "I Have Loved You Girl (But Not Like This Before)," Earl Thomas Conley

Barbara Mandrell

347. Barbara Mandrell had 25 records chart before she finally had a #1 single. What record took her all the way to the top?
A) "Do Right Woman—Do Right Man"
B) "The Midnight Oil"
C) "Married but Not to Each Other"
D) "Sleeping Single in a Double Bed"

348. What song do Kenny Chesney and his girlfriend sing on the hood of his car in "Don't Happen Twice"?
A) "Afternoon Delight"
B) "Cheap Sunglasses"
C) "Me and Bobby McGee"
D) "Proud Mary"

349. What was Tim McGraw's first Top Ten hit?
A) "Don't Take the Girl"
B) "Down on the Farm"
C) "Indian Outlaw"
D) "Not a Moment Too Soon"

Answers begin on page 169.

350. In which Highway 101 video does rockabilly great Carl Perkins have a cameo?

A) "Cry, Cry, Cry"

B) "Honky Tonk Heart"

C) "Walkin', Talkin', Cryin', Barely Beatin' Broken Heart"

D) "Bing, Bang, Boom"

351. What Confederate Railroad video features Grand Ole Opry stars Stonewall Jackson and Jeannie Seely as the parents of singer Danny Shirley?

A) "Daddy Never Was the Cadillac Kind"   C) "Summer in Dixie"

B) "Queen of Memphis"   D) "Trashy Women"

352. Which song made Tim McGraw smile by topping the charts in 1998?

A) "Just to See You Smile"   C) "She'll Leave You with a Smile"

B) "Mona Lisa Lost Her Smile"   D) "Smile"

353. Which song gave Mel McDaniel his only #1 hit?

A) "Baby's Got Her Blue Jeans On"   C) "Jeans On"

B) "Between Blue Eyes and Jeans"   D) "Make-Up and Faded Blue Jeans"

354. Which of these songs helped Blake Shelton break through in 2001?

A) "Abilene"   B) "Austin"   C) "Dallas"   D) "Laredo"

355. Which of these songs, all hits for Mel Tillis during the 1960s, later gave Ricky Van Shelton a #1 record?

A) "All Right (I'll Sign the Papers)"   C) "These Lonely Hands of Mine"

B) "Life Turned Her That Way"   D) "Who's Julie"

356. What Alan Jackson record is playing on the jukebox at the beginning of Jackson's "Chasin' That Neon Rainbow" video?

A) "Blue Blooded Woman"   C) "I'd Love You All Over Again"

B) "Don't Rock the Jukebox"   D) "Wanted"

357. What Judds video was shot in 3-D?

A) "Give a Little Love"

B) "Grandpa (Tell Me 'bout the Good Old Days)"

C) "Love Can Build a Bridge"

D) "Mama He's Crazy"

Answers begin on page 169.

358. In which Patty Loveless video did actor David Keith play her love interest?
A) "Blame It on Your Heart"   C) "The Night's Too Long"
B) "If My Heart Had Windows"   D) "Hurt Me Bad (In a Real Good Way)"

359. Which song was a Trace Adkins hit?
A) "(This Ain't) No Thinkin' Thing"   C) "Thinkin' Problem"
B) "Thinkin' about You"   D) "What Were You Thinkin'"

360. Which of these songs was a #1 hit for Rhett Akins?
A) "Don't Get Me Started"
B) "Finish What We Started"
C) "Let's Get Started If We're Going to Break My Heart"
D) "She Just Started Liking Cheatin' Songs"

361. Alabama had a hit with which of these songs?
A) "Brother Jukebox"   C) "Prop Me Up beside the Jukebox (If I Die)"
B) "Jukebox in My Mind"   D) "Put a Quarter in the Jukebox"

362. What song was Gary Allan's first hit?
A) "Her Man"   C) "Man of Me"
B) "No Man in His Wrong Heart"   D) "Man to Man"

363. Which of these hits did Bill Anderson sing?
A) "Still"   C) "Still in Love with You"
B) "Still Doin' Time"   D) "Still Loving You"

364. What Sawyer Brown video features banjo great Earl Scruggs?
A) "The Boys & Me"   B) "The Dirt Road"   C) "Six Days on the Road"   D) "The Walk"

365. In which Hank Williams Jr. video are members of the rock group Van Halen among his guests?
A) "All My Rowdy Friends Are Coming Over Tonight"
B) "If It Will It Will"
C) "My Name Is Bocephus"
D) "Young Country"

366. Which song did Lynn Anderson take to the top of the charts?
A) "Rose Bouquet"   B) "Rose Garden"   C) "Roses and Thorns"   D) "Roses for Mama"

Answers begin on page 169.

367. Which song did Glen Campbell take to the top of the country charts?

A) "Southern Loving" C) "Southern Rains"
B) "Southern Nights" D) "Southern Star"

368. What song topped the charts for John Anderson?

A) "He Drinks Tequila" C) "Tequila Sunrise"
B) "Straight Tequila Night" D) "Tequila Talkin'"

369. Which song rose to the top of the charts for John Conlee?

A) "The Rose" C) "Rose in Paradise"
B) "Rose-Colored Glasses" D) "Roses and Love Songs"

370. Which Dwight Yoakam video co-stars actors Harry Dean Stanton and Bo Hopkins?

A) "Gone (That'll Be Me)" C) "Pocket of a Clown"
B) "Nothing" D) "Sorry You Asked"

371. Which of these songs was not a hit for Bobby Bare?

A) "Detroit City" C) "How I Got to Memphis"
B) "The Streets of Baltimore" D) "Saginaw, Michigan"

372. Which of these songs was Alan Jackson's first Top Forty hit?

A) "Here in the Real World" C) "A World without Love"
B) "I'll Leave This World Loving You" D) "What's Going on in Your World"

373. Which song was a Tracy Lawrence hit?

A) "Honky Tonk World" C) "Rock My World (Little Country Girl)"
B) "If the World Had a Front Porch" D) "Today My World Slipped Away"

374. Which song was a Top Ten hit for Asleep at the Wheel?

A) "(Love Always) Letter to Home" C) "Tear-Stained Letter"
B) "Take a Letter Maria" D) "The Letter That Johnny Walker Read"

375. What 1973 pop hit for B.W. Stevenson did Brooks & Dunn cover and take to #1 on the country charts?

A) "She Used to Be Mine" C) "My Maria"
B) "That Ain't No Way to Go" D) "You're Gonna Miss Me When I'm Gone"

Answers begin on page 169.

376. **Which of these songs was a Top Five hit for David Ball?**
    A) "Drinkin' Thing"
    B) "Drinkin' My Baby Goodbye"
    C) "Thinkin' Problem"
    D) "What Were You Thinkin'"

377. **Which BlackHawk hit was written by Shania Twain's husband?**
    A) "Every Once in a While"
    B) "I Sure Can Smell the Rain"
    C) "I'm Not Strong Enough to Say No"
    D) "There You Have It"

378. **Baillie & the Boys had a hit with which of these songs?**
    A) "Hearts of Stone"
    B) "(I Wish I Had a) Heart of Stone"
    C) "Let Go of the Stone"
    D) "Steppin' Stone"

379. **With which song did Johnny Bush have a Top Ten hit in 1969?**
    A) "High on a Mountain Top"
    B) "Mountain of Love"
    C) "Wolverton Mountain"
    D) "You Gave Me a Mountain"

380. **Moe Bandy had a hit with which of these songs about Hank Williams?**
    A) "Hank and Lefty Raised My Country Soul"
    B) "Hank Williams, You Wrote My Life"
    C) "The Night Hank Williams Came to Town"
    D) "I Feel Like Hank Williams Tonight"

381. **With which of these songs did the Bellamy Brothers top the charts?**
    A) "Do You Love As Good As You Look"
    B) "You Look So Good in Love"
    C) "You Look Like the One I Love"
    D) "You Can't Keep a Good Memory Down"

382. **What was Clint Black's debut single?**
    A) "A Better Man"
    B) "Better Man, Better Off"
    C) "Better Move It on Home"
    D) "Better Things to Do"

383. **Which song, written by John Hiatt, was a hit for Suzy Bogguss?**
    A) "Drive South"
    B) "True Believer"
    C) "She Don't Love Nobody"
    D) "The Way We Make a Broken Heart"

384. **Which of these songs was the only chart-topping hit for Lionel Cartwright?**
    A) "Faith in Me, Faith in You"
    B) "Faith in You"
    C) "Have a Little Faith"
    D) "Leap of Faith"

Answers begin on page 169.

385. **What Bill Monroe song was a #1 hit for Eddy Arnold in 1951?**
A) "Kentucky Waltz"   B) "Oklahoma Waltz"   C) "Tennessee Waltz"   D) "Waltz across Texas"

386. **Which song was Dave & Sugar's first hit?**
A) "Queen of Hearts"
B) "Queen of Honky Tonk Street"
C) "Queen of the House"
D) "Queen of the Silver Dollar"

387. **With which song did Gail Davies have a Top Ten hit?**
A) "Round About Way"
B) "'Round Here"
C) "'Round the Clock Lovin'"
D) "Round-Up Saloon"

388. **What song, written by Lucinda Williams, was a hit for Mary Chapin Carpenter?**
A) "Always Late with Your Kisses"
B) "Butterfly Kisses"
C) "Cover You in Kisses"
D) "Passionate Kisses"

389. **According to *Billboard*, what was Vince Gill's first #1 single?**
A) "Oklahoma Borderline"
B) "When I Call Your Name"
C) "Pocket Full of Gold"
D) "I Still Believe in You"

Vince Gill

390. **What was Carl & Pearl Butler's only #1 hit?**
A) "Don't Let Me Cross Over"
B) "Loving Arms"
C) "Too Late to Try Again"
D) "I'm Hanging up the Phone"

391. **Which song did Jeff Carson take to the top spot on the country charts?**
A) "How Your Love Makes Me Feel"
B) "It's Your Love"
C) "Not on Your Love"
D) "Your Love Amazes Me"

392. **Which of Mac Davis's country hits placed highest on the pop charts?**
A) "Baby Don't Get Hooked on Me"
B) "Hooked on Music"
C) "It's Hard to Be Humble"
D) "Rock 'N' Roll (I Gave You the Best Years of My Life)"

Answers begin on page 169.

393. **Carlene Carter had a Top Five hit with which song?**
A) "Crazy Little Thing Called Love"   C) "Little Things"
B) "Every Little Thing"   D) "The Sweetest Thing"

394. **Which of these songs did Johnny Duncan take to the top of the charts?**
A) "Think about Love"   C) "Thinkin' of a Rendezvous"
B) "Think of Me"   D) "Thinking 'bout You, Babe"

395. **Which song was a hit for Stoney Edwards?**
A) "Hank and Lefty Raised My Country Soul"   C) "Hank Williams's Guitar"
B) "Hank Drank"   D) "Hank Williams, You Wrote My Life"

396. **Which Cledus T. Judd record was not a spoof of a country hit?**
A) "Did I Shave My Back for This?"   C) "How Do You Milk a Cow"
B) "Everybody's Free (to Get Sunburned)"   D) "My Cellmate Thinks I'm Sexy"

397. **Which of these chart-topping hits did Deana Carter record?**
A) "Could I Have This Dance"
B) "I Can Tell by the Way You Dance (You're Gonna Love Me Tonight)"
C) "We Danced"
D) "We Danced Anyway"

398. **Which song put Chad Brock in the Top Five for the first time?**
A) "Ordinary Life"   C) "Ordinary People"
B) "Ordinary Love"   D) "She Ain't Your Ordinary Girl"

399. **With what song, initially a 1970s hit for Hank Williams Jr., did Mark Chesnutt hit #1?**
A) "Eleven Roses"   C) "The Last Love Song"
B) "I'll Think of Something"   D) "Pride's Not Hard to Swallow"

400. **Which song was a Roy Clark hit?**
A) "Yesterday"   C) "Yesterday Once More"
B) "Yesterday, When I Was Young"   D) "Yesterday's Wine"

401. **Which of these songs did Crystal Gayle take to #1?**
A) "'Til I Can Make It on My Own"   C) "'Til I Gain Control Again"
B) "'Til I Can't Take It Anymore"   D) "'Til Love Comes Again"

*Answers begin on page 169.

402. Janie Fricke topped the charts with which song?
A) "He's a Heartache (Looking for a Place to Happen)"
B) "It's a Heartache"
C) "Let the Heartache Ride"
D) "Ridin' Out the Heartache"

403. Don Gibson had a #1 hit with which of these songs?
A) "Blue Bayou"   B) "Blue Blue Day"   C) "Blue Boy"   D) "Blue Heartache"

404. Which Lonestar hit mentions the rock group Pearl Jam?
A) "Tequila Talkin'"
B) "No News"
C) "Come Cryin' to Me"
D) "Runnin' Away with My Heart"

405. Which song did Sammy Kershaw drive to the Top Five?
A) "Cadillac Ranch"
B) "Cadillac Style"
C) "Cadillac Tears"
D) "Daddy Never Was the Cadillac Kind"

406. With which of these songs did Earl Thomas Conley have a #1 single?
A) "Blue Moon"
B) "Does That Blue Moon Ever Shine on You"
C) "Ohce in a Blue Moon"
D) "Once in a Very Blue Moon"

407. Which song was Cowboy Copas's signature hit?
A) "Alabam"
B) "Alabama Jubilee"
C) "Alabama Summertime"
D) "Alabama Wild Man"

408. Billy "Crash" Craddock had a #1 hit with which of these songs?
A) "Ruby Ann"
B) "Ruby, Baby"
C) "Ruby, Don't Take Your Love to Town"
D) "Ruby You're Warm"

409. Which of Mickey Gilley's #1 hits was a remake of a song by r&b singer Sam Cooke?
A) "Bring It on Home to Me"
B) "Stand by Me"
C) "Talk to Me"
D) "True Love Ways"

410. Which song was a chart-topping hit for Jack Guthrie & His Oklahomans?
A) "Oklahoma Borderline"
B) "Oklahoma Hills"
C) "Oklahoma Sunday Morning"
D) "Oklahoma Waltz"

*Answers begin on page 169.

411. Which song was a Top Twenty hit for both its writer, Wynn Stewart, and his one-time bass player, Merle Haggard?

A) "Sing a Sad Song"
B) "Sing Me Back Home"
C) "Singer of Sad Songs"
D) "Singing the Blues"

412. What song was Billy Ray Cyrus's follow-up single to "Achy Breaky Heart"?

A) "Could've Been Me"
B) "It Could've Been So Good"
C) "You Could've Had Me"
D) "You Could've Heard a Heart Break"

413. Which song was a hit for Billy Dean?

A) "For My Broken Heart"
B) "Like We Never Had a Broken Heart"
C) "My Next Broken Heart"
D) "Somewhere in My Broken Heart"

Crystal Gayle

414. What song gave Crystal Gayle her first #1 record, and was the first song by writer Richard Leigh ever to be recorded?

A) "Wrong Road Again"
B) "I'll Get Over You"
C) "Your Old Cold Shoulder"
D) "Don't It Make My Brown Eyes Blue"

415. Boxer George Foreman appears in which George Jones video?

A) "High-Tech Redneck"
B) "Honky Tonk Song"
C) "I Don't Need Your Rockin' Chair"
D) "Wrong's What I Do Best"

416. Which song topped the charts for Diamond Rio?

A) "Another Day of Loving"
B) "A Good Day to Run"
C) "One More Day"
D) "What a Beautiful Day"

417. Which song was a hit for Highway 101?

A) "Good Friends, Good Whiskey, Good Lovin'"
B) "Cheap Whiskey"
C) "Wake Up and Smell the Whiskey"
D) "Whiskey, If You Were a Woman"

Answers begin on page 169.

418. What was the Dixie Chicks' first hit single?
A) "I Can Love You Better" C) "There's Your Trouble"
B) "Ready to Run" D) "Wide Open Spaces"

419. Which of these Emmylou Harris records wasn't a remake of an older pop hit?
A) "Born to Run" C) "Save the Last Dance for Me"
B) "Pledging My Love" D) "(You Never Can Tell) C'est la Vie"

420. What song entered the charts just days before Hawkshaw Hawkins's death and posthumously gave him his only #1 hit?
A) "Dog House Boogie" C) "Slow Poke"
B) "I Love You a Thousand Ways" D) "Lonesome 7-7203"

421. What was Joe Diffie's debut single?
A) "Home" C) "Home Sweet Home"
B) "Home Again in My Heart" D) "Home to You"

422. What was Holly Dunn's first Top Ten hit?
A) "Daddy What If" C) "Daddy's Hands"
B) "Daddy's Come Around" D) "Daddy's Money"

423. Steve Earle had a Top Ten hit with which of these songs?
A) "Big Guitar" B) "Guitar Man" C) "Guitar Town" D) "Rhythm Guitar"

424. Which song was a hit for SHeDAISY?
A) "Goodbye Says It All" C) "Standing on the Edge of Goodbye"
B) "Little Good-Byes" D) "Goodbye on a Bad Day"

425. Which song became a patriotic standard after Lee Greenwood made it a hit?
A) "American Made"
B) "God Bless America Again"
C) "God Bless the U.S.A."
D) "There's a Star-Spangled Banner Waving Somewhere"

426. With which song did Exile reach the top of the charts?
A) "Chance of Lovin' You" C) "I Didn't (Every Chance I Had)"
B) "Give Me One More Chance" D) "One More Last Chance"

*Answers begin on page 169.

427. **What song was a Top Ten hit for Johnny Horton in the 1950s and for George Jones in the 1980s?**
    A) "All Grown Up"
    B) "Honky-Tonk Man"
    C) "I'm a One-Woman Man"
    D) "The Woman I Need"

428. **The Forester Sisters had a chart-topping record with which of these songs?**
    A) "Mama Knows"
    B) "Mama Knows the Highway"
    C) "Mama He's Crazy"
    D) "Mama's Never Seen Those Eyes"

429. **What song gave duo Foster & Lloyd a Top Five hit with its first single?**
    A) "Crazy for Your Love"
    B) "Crazy in Love"
    C) "Crazy Over You"
    D) "She's Crazy for Leaving"

430. **With what song did Radney Foster have his first hit after leaving Foster & Lloyd?**
    A) "High Lonesome Sound"
    B) "Just Call Me Lonesome"
    C) "Lonesome Standard Time"
    D) "A Real Good Way to Wind Up Lonesome"

431. **David Frizzell & Shelly West had their first #1 hit with which song?**
    A) "Oklahoma Borderline"
    B) "Oklahoma Swing"
    C) "Tokyo, Oklahoma"
    D) "You're the Reason God Made Oklahoma"

432. **Which song was a hit for Larry Gatlin?**
    A) "Night Games"
    B) "Night Is Fallin' in My Heart"
    C) "Night Time and My Baby"
    D) "Night Time Magic"

433. **Which song, penned by George Jones, gave Stonewall Jackson his first hit?**
    A) "Life's Like Poetry"
    B) "Life of a Poor Boy"
    C) "Life to Go"
    D) "Life Turned Her That Way"

434. **Which of Waylon Jennings's hits did Rodney Crowell write?**
    A) "Amanda"
    B) "I Ain't Living Long Like This"
    C) "Rose in Paradise"
    D) "Lucille (You Won't Do Your Daddy's Will)"

435. **What song gave Wade Hayes a #1 hit with his first single for Columbia Records?**
    A) "I've Been Around Enough to Know"
    B) "Much Too Young (to Feel This Damn Old)"
    C) "Old Enough to Know Better"
    D) "Strong Enough to Bend"

Answers begin on page 169.

436. Which song was a Vince Gill hit?

A) "Band of Gold"
B) "Everything That Glitters (Is Not Gold)"
C) "House of Gold"
D) "Pocket Full of Gold"

437. Vern Gosdin had a hit with which of these songs?

A) "A Man Ain't Made of Stone"
B) "Chiseled in Stone"
C) "Let Go of the Stone"
D) "Stone Cold Country"

438. What record won Jack Greene the Country Music Association's Single of the Year award in 1967?

A) "There Goes My Baby"
B) "There Goes My Everything"
C) "There Goes My Heart"
D) "There Goes My Love"

439. Sara Evans flew to the top of the charts with which of these songs?

A) "Born to Fly"
B) "Fly"
C) "Fly Away"
D) "Why Walk When You Can Fly"

440. What was Faith Hill's first single?

A) "Let's Go to Vegas"
B) "Piece of My Heart"
C) "Take Me As I Am"
D) "Wild One"

441. Under which title did the Marcy Brothers record the song that would, just one year later, become a million-selling hit for Billy Ray Cyrus?

A) "Aching, Breaking Heart"
B) "Achy Breaky Heart"
C) "Don't Tell My Heart"
D) "You Can Tell the World"

442. Which of these cheating songs wasn't a hit for the Kendalls?

A) "Cheater's Prayer"
B) "Don't Cheat in Our Hometown"
C) "Teach Me to Cheat"
D) "You'd Make an Angel Want to Cheat"

443. Which Bruce Springsteen song was a Top Twenty country hit for Chris LeDoux?

A) "All That Heaven Will Allow"
B) "Cadillac Ranch"
C) "Pink Cadillac"
D) "Tougher Than the Rest"

444. Which of these songs did Michael Johnson take to the top of the country charts?

A) "Rope The Moon"
B) "Sad-Lookin' Moon"
C) "Talkin' to the Moon"
D) "The Moon Is Still over Her Shoulder"

*Answers begin on page 169.

445. **What was Ty Herndon's debut single?**
A) "No Matter How High"   C) "All That Matters Anymore"
B) "It Matters to Me"   D) "What Mattered Most"

446. **Which of these songs isn't a Tom T. Hall hit?**
A) "I Believe in You"   B) "I Care"   C) "I Like Beer"   D) "I Love"

447. **Randy Travis and Sonny James both topped the country charts by covering which of pop singer Brook Benton's records?**
A) "Endlessly"   C) "It's Just a Matter of Time"
B) "Going Going Gone"   D) "Rainy Night in Georgia"

448. **What was the first Jerry Lee Lewis single to make the country charts?**
A) "Whole Lot of Shakin' Going On"
B) "Breathless"
C) "What's Made Milwaukee Famous (Has Made a Loser out of Me)"
D) "Middle Age Crazy"

449. **Which Bob Luman hit later became a hit for Luman's one-time band member Steve Wariner?**
A) "Let's Think about Living"   C) "Still Loving You"
B) "Lonely Women Make Good Lovers"   D) "Just Enough to Make Me Stay"

450. **What was Loretta Lynn's first Top Ten hit?**
A) "Success"
B) "Don't Come Home A'Drinkin' (with Lovin' on Your Mind)"
C) "Coal Miner's Daughter"
D) "Fist City"

451. **Which Kathy Mattea hit won her Single of the Year awards from both the Academy of Country Music and the Country Music Association?**
A) "Come from the Heart"   C) "Love at the Five & Dime"
B) "Eighteen Wheels and a Dozen Roses" D) "Where've You Been"

452. **Which song was a #1 hit for Toby Keith?**
A) "Kiss This"   C) "Let's Make Sure We Kiss Goodbye"
B) "Kiss Me in the Car"   D) "You Shouldn't Kiss Me Like This"

Answers begin on page 169.

453. Which song was Hal Ketchum's first hit?
A) "Jukebox Saturday Night"
B) "Louisiana Saturday Night"
C) "Small Town Saturday Night"
D) "Tennessee Saturday Night"

454. Which Keith Whitley hit did Alison Krauss & Union Station revive in 1995?
A) "Don't Close Your Eyes"
B) "I Wonder Do You Think of Me"
C) "I'm No Stranger to the Rain"
D) "When You Say Nothing at All"

455. Tracy Lawrence topped the charts with which of these songs?
A) "Texas in My Rear View Mirror"
B) "Texas Tattoo"
C) "Texas Tornado"
D) "Texas Women"

456. Which of these songs was a hit for both Eddy Arnold and Ray Price?
A) "Make the World Go Away"
B) "Turn the World Around"
C) "Welcome to My World"
D) "What's He Doing in My World"

457. What K.T. Oslin single was inspired by a piece of bathroom-wall graffiti?
A) "Come Next Monday"
B) "Cornell Crawford"
C) "I'll Always Come Back"
D) "Wall of Tears"

Tim McGraw

458. What song did Tim McGraw take to #1 in 1999 after it had failed to break the Top Forty for writer Rodney Crowell four years earlier?
A) "For a Little While"
B) "Please Remember Me"
C) "Something Like That"
D) "My Best Friend"

459. What George Jones hit later became Patty Loveless's first Top Ten hit?
A) "If My Heart Had Windows"
B) "A Picture of Me (Without You)"
C) "The Window Up Above"
D) "Walk Through this World with Me"

460. What Keith Whitley record was on the charts at the time of his death on May 9, 1989?
A) "Don't Close Your Eyes"
B) "Hard Livin'"
C) "I Wonder Do You Think of Me"
D) "I'm No Stranger to the Rain"

Answers begin on page 169.

461. Which of these Glen Campbell hits was not written by Jimmy Webb?
A) "By the Time I Get to Phoenix"　　C) "Southern Nights"
B) "Galveston"　　D) "Wichita Lineman"

462. What Michael Martin Murphey song was a pop hit in 1975 and a country hit in 1985?
A) "Carolina in the Pines"　　C) "What's Forever For"
B) "What Am I Doing Hangin' 'Round?"　　D) "Wildfire"

463. Which song was Lyle Lovett's only Top Ten country hit?
A) "Cowboy Band"　　C) "Should've Been a Cowboy"
B) "Cowboy Man"　　D) "Whatcha Gonna Do with a Cowboy"

464. Which song was Martina McBride's first #1 hit?
A) "Angels among Us"　　C) "Ten Thousand Angels"
B) "Concrete Angel"　　D) "Wild Angels"

465. What was Jo Dee Messina's first single?
A) "Bye-Bye"　　C) "Stand beside Me"
B) "Heads Carolina, Tails California"　　D) "You're Not in Kansas Anymore"

466. Which Reba McEntire single is considered to be the first country hit to broach the subject of AIDS?
A) "For My Broken Heart"　　C) "Rumor Has It"
B) "The Heart Is a Lonely Hunter"　　D) "She Thinks His Name Was John"

467. What Hoagy Carmichael song was a #1 pop hit for Ray Charles in 1960 and a #1 country hit for Willie Nelson in 1978?
A) "All of Me"　　C) "I Can't Stop Loving You"
B) "Georgia on My Mind"　　D) "Stardust"

468. What 1992 video featured future Oscar-winning actress Mira Sorvino?
A) "Working Woman," Rob Crosby　　C) "Suspicious Minds," Dwight Yoakam
B) "Poisoned at the Well," Bob Woodruff　　D) "Past the Point of Rescue," Hal Ketchum

469. Which Lari White video caused an uproar in the mental-health community over its depiction of the mentally ill?
A) "That's My Baby"　　C) "Stepping Stone"
B) "Now I Know"　　D) "Wild at Heart"

Answers begin on page 169.

470. **Which Alabama video did RCA Records recall because the group's management considered it too racy?**
   A) "Can't Keep a Good Man Down"
   C) "(There's a) Fire in the Night"
   B) "Hometown Honeymoon"
   D) "Touch Me When We're Dancing"

471. **What Suzy Bogguss video co-starred Billy Dean, who, at the time, was still more than a year away from his first hit?**
   A) "Cross My Broken Heart"
   C) "Someday Soon"
   B) "My Sweet Love Ain't Around"
   D) "Somewhere Between"

472. **In which Nanci Griffith video does Lyle Lovett appear as one of Griffith's backup singers?**
   A) "Once in a Very Blue Moon"
   C) "Trouble in the Fields"
   B) "Lone Star State of Mind"
   D) "Cold Hearts/Closed Minds"

473. **What was the first country video to be shown on MTV?**
   A) "All My Rowdy Friends Are Coming Over Tonight," Hank Williams Jr.
   B) "God Bless the U.S.A.," Lee Greenwood
   C) "Planet Texas," Kenny Rogers
   D) "Step by Step," Eddie Rabbitt

474. **What Johnny Cash video featured model Kate Moss?**
   A) "Delia's Gone"   B) "Drive On"   C) "Johnny 99"   D) "Rusty Cage"

475. **In which George Jones video does producer Billy Sherrill appear as a bus driver?**
   A) "Who's Gonna Fill Their Shoes"
   C) "You Couldn't Get the Picture"
   B) "The Old Man No One Loves"
   D) "She Loved a Lot in Her Time"

476. **What song plays on a truck radio in Shenandoah's video for "The Church on Cumberland Road"?**
   A) "Mama Knows"
   C) "Sunday in the South"
   B) "She Doesn't Cry Anymore"
   D) "Two Dozen Roses"

477. **Which of his hits had Ferlin Husky recorded ten years earlier under the name Terry Preston?**
   A) "Gone"
   B) "I Feel Better All Over (More Than Anywhere's Else)"
   C) "A Fallen Star"
   D) "Wings of a Dove"

*Answers begin on page 169.

Kenny Chesney

478. **Kenny Chesney climbed to the top of the charts with which of these songs?**
A) "She's Got a Man on Her Mind"
B) "She's Got It All"
C) "She's Got That Look in Her Eyes"
D) "She's Got the Rhythm (and I Got the Blues)"

479. **Tracy Byrd had his first #1 hit with which of these songs?**
A) "A Man Holdin' On (to a Woman Lettin' Go)"
B) "Heaven in My Woman's Eyes"
C) "Holdin'"
D) "Holdin' Heaven"

480. **What future Brenda Lee hit was on the demo that got Loretta Lynn signed to Decca Records?**
A) "All Alone Am I"
B) "Break It to Me Gently"
C) "Everybody Loves Me but You"
D) "Fool #1"

481. **What Garth Brooks video initially was banned by CMT for its portrayal of domestic violence?**
A) "Papa Loved Mama"
B) "The River"
C) "The Thunder Rolls"
D) "Two of a Kind, Workin' on a Full House"

482. **These four actors placed these singles on the country charts—but only one reached the Top Ten. Which one?**
A) Lorne Green, "Ringo"
B) Robert Mitchum, "Little Old Wine Drinker Me"
C) Vicki Lawrence, "The Night the Lights Went Out in Georgia"
D) George Burns, "I Wish I Was Eighteen Again"

483. **Which song was Kitty Wells's famous answer song, "It Wasn't God Who Made Honky Tonk Angels," answering?**
A) "The Wild Side of Life"
B) "Honky Tonk Angels"
C) "Close Up the Honky Tonks"
D) "Dim Lights, Thick Smoke, and Loud, Loud Music"

Answers begin on page 169.

484. What Queen song did Dwight Yoakam record for a Gap commercial?

A) "Another One Bites the Dust"
B) "Bohemian Rhapsody"
C) "Crazy Little Thing Called Love"
D) "Fat Bottomed Girls"

485. On what chart-topping country record did Red Foley sing with Lawrence Welk & His Orchestra?

A) "Have I Told You Lately That I Love You"
B) "Hang Your Head in Shame"
C) "Shame on You"
D) "Smoke on the Water"

486. In what Alan Jackson video did Keith Urban appear as a guitar player?

A) "Don't Rock the Jukebox"
B) "Little Man"
C) "Mercury Blues"
D) "Right on the Money"

487. What song, best known as a George Strait hit, did Country Music Hall of Famer Merle Haggard record on his 1986 album *Out Among the Stars*?

A) "Don't Make Me Come Over There and Love You"
B) "Tell Me Something Bad about Tulsa"
C) "The Chill of an Early Fall"
D) "What Do You Say to That"

488. On which of these songs does Don Schlitz not have a writer's credit?

A) "Forever and Ever, Amen"
B) "He Walked on Water"
C) "On the Other Hand"
D) "The Gambler"

489. What was Rick Treviño's only #1 hit?

A) "She Can't Say I Didn't Cry"
B) "Doctor Time"
C) "Learning as You Go"
D) "Running out of Reasons to Run"

490. What was Billy Walker's only #1 hit?

A) "Charlie's Shoes"
B) "A Million and One"
C) "Cross the Brazos at Waco"
D) "Bear with Me a Little Longer"

491. What Harlan Howard song was a Top Five hit in 1966 for his wife at the time, Jan Howard?

A) "Evil Angel"
B) "Evil off My Mind"
C) "Evil on Your Mind"
D) "Leavin' on Your Mind"

*Answers begin on page 169.

492. **What Con Hunley single was later covered by Alan Jackson on his 1999 *Under the Influence* album?**
A) "All-American Country Boy"
B) "I've Been Waiting for You All of My Life"
C) "Oh Girl"
D) "What's New with You"

493. **Which of Elvis Presley's early hits did the Judds remake and take to the Top Ten?**
A) "Don't Be Cruel"
B) "Heartbreak Hotel"
C) "Love Me"
D) "Let Me Be Your Teddy Bear"

494. **What song by rock group Los Lobos did Waylon Jennings turn into a country hit in 1986?**
A) "Don't Worry Baby"
B) "I Got Loaded"
C) "One Time One Night"
D) "Will the Wolf Survive?"

495. **What's the lowest-charting single to win the Country Music Association's Single of the Year award?**
A) "I Am a Man of Constant Sorrow," The Soggy Bottom Boys
B) "When You Say Nothing at All," Alison Krauss & Union Station
C) "I'm No Stranger to the Rain," Keith Whitley
D) "Country Bumpkin," Cal Smith

Answers begin on page 169.

— NAME THAT SONG ANSWERS —

1. C) "The Devil Went Down to Georgia"—"The Devil Went Down to Georgia" spent one week atop the country chart in August 1979.

2. C) "Don't Be Cruel," Elvis Presley—"Don't Be Cruel" spent ten weeks atop the country chart, eleven weeks atop the pop chart, and six at #1 on the r&b chart.

3. A) "I'm Already There"

4. C) "Hard Luck Woman"—The members of Kiss back Brooks on the track.

5. D) "Stand by Your Man"

6. C) "Help Me Make It through the Night"

7. D) "Queen of My Double Wide Trailer," Sammy Kershaw—In the song, Earl is referred to as "the Charlie Daniels of the torque wrench."

8. D) "The Ballad of Jed Clampett," Flatt & Scruggs—"The Ballad of Jed Clampett," also known as the theme from CBS-TV's *The Beverly Hillbillies*, spent three weeks at #1 in early 1963, during the show's first season.

9. C) "Slipping Around"—Songwriter Floyd Tillman also charted with "Slipping Around" that year, but his version climbed only to #5.

10. D) "Heartbreak Hotel"

11. C) "Islands in the Stream"

12. D) "Uncle Pen"

13. C) "Down the Road Mountain Pass"—"Down the Road Mountain Pass," from Fogelberg's bluegrass-inspired *High Country Snows*, featured such musicians as Ricky Skaggs and Jerry Douglas and reached #33 in 1985.

14. A) "Big Train (from Memphis)"—"Big Train (from Memphis)" was the flip side of "The Old Man Down the Road," a Top Ten pop hit.

15. A) "It's Like We Never Said Goodbye," Crystal Gayle—West's, Boone's and Harris's singles would all top the charts in subsequent weeks. Wynette's "Two Story House"—actually a duet with George Jones—peaked at #2.

16. A) "Willingly," with Shirley Collie—"Willingly," a 1962 Top Ten single, was not only Nelson's first duet hit, it was his first record to reach the Top Forty.

17. C) "It Wasn't God Who Made Honky Tonk Angels," Kitty Wells—"It Wasn't God Who Made Honky Tonk Angels" reached #1 August 23, 1952.

18. D) "Take These Chains from My Heart"—Williams flew to Shreveport, Louisiana, after the session and never returned to Nashville. Fifteen weeks later, he was dead.
19. D) "Stand by Me"
20. C) "Fancy"
21. C) "Stand by Your Man," Tammy Wynette—"Stand by Your Man," Wynette's only Top Forty pop hit, stalled at #19 on the pop charts. "Ode to Billie Joe," however, was the only one of the four singles that didn't top the country chart, peaking at #17.
22. A) "Gotta Travel On," Billy Grammer
23. B) "He'll Have to Go"
24. D) "Somewhere in the Vicinity of the Heart"
25. A) "Blue Christmas"
26. A) "City Lights"—Price's version of the song topped the charts in 1958, Gilley's in 1975.
27. C) "Tennessee Flat Top Box"
28. A) "Ashes by Now"
29. A) "Always on My Mind"—Willie's version of "Always on My Mind" won the Country Music Association's Single of the Year award in 1982.
30. B) "Piece of My Heart"—"Piece of My Heart" was a #12 pop hit for the Joplin-fronted Big Brother and the Holding Company in 1968 and a #10 r&b hit for Erma Franklin, Aretha's sister, in 1967.
31. A) "Cry! Cry! Cry!"
32. A) "Am I Losing You"
33. A) "Don't Let the Stars Get in Your Eyes"
34. B) "Folsom Prison Blues"—Cash's 1968 version actually was recorded in Folsom Prison.
35. B) "Honky Tonkin'"—"Honky Tonkin'" was a #1 hit for Hank Williams Jr. in 1982. His daddy's version got to #14.
36. A) "Good Hearted Woman"
37. D) "You Had Me from Hello"
38. B) "Act Naturally"
39. C) "I Forgot to Remember to Forget"
40. A) "Should've Been a Cowboy"
41. A) "She's in Love with the Boy"

42. B) "I Will Always Love You"
43. A) "Does He Love You"
44. C) "Farewell Party"—Watson's backing band is known as the Farewell Party Band.
45. B) "I'm So Lonesome I Could Cry"
46. C) "Friends in Low Places"—Dewayne Blackwell and Earl "Bud" Lee penned the award-winning song.
47. A) "Here in the Real World"—Jackson wrote the song with Mark Irwin.
48. C) "Wabash Cannon Ball"—"Wabash Cannon Ball" was one of Roy Acuff's signature tunes.
49. B) "The Gambler"—Don Schlitz penned Kenny Rogers's 1978 chart-topper.
50. D) "Sixteen Tons"—Written by Merle Travis, "Sixteen Tons" was a massive hit for Tennessee Ernie Ford in 1955 and 1956.
51. B) "The Battle of New Orleans"—"The Battle of New Orleans" was a 1959 hit for both Johnny Horton and the song's writer, Jimmie Driftwood.
52. D) "Gentle on My Mind"
53. D) "Daydream Believer"
54. B) "The Fever"
55. D) "Walkin' after Midnight"
56. C) "I'm So Happy I Can't Stop Crying"
57. B) "Walkaway Joe"
58. B) "It's Your Love"
59. A) "Blue Blooded Woman"—The single failed to reach the Top Forty.
60. D) "To Make You Feel My Love"
61. D) "You Never Even Called Me by My Name"
62. B) "If Tomorrow Never Comes"
63. B) "Easy Loving"
64. D) "Walk Softly on This Heart of Mine"
65. B) "From Graceland to the Promised Land"
66. C) "Blue Eyes Crying in the Rain"—"Blue Eyes Crying in the Rain" was written by Acuff-Rose Publications co-founder Fred Rose.
67. C) "May the Bird of Paradise Fly up Your Nose"
68. B) "Jackson"—The 1967 single won a Grammy for the couple, who would marry in March 1968.

69. A) "If My Heart Had Windows"
70. D) "She's Got the Rhythm (and I Got the Blues)"—Jackson and Travis also collaborated for the Travis hits "Forever Together" and "Better Class of Losers."
71. A) "Any Man of Mine"
72. D) "Choices"—Jackson sang "Choices" in honor of George Jones, who declined to perform after he was told he wouldn't be able to sing the entire song on the show.
73. B) "If You Ain't Lovin' (You Ain't Livin')"
74. B) "City of New Orleans"—"City of New Orleans," also a pop hit for Arlo Guthrie, was written by Steve Goodman.
75. A) "Cold, Cold Heart"
76. A) "(I'm a Lonesome) Fugitive"—Though Haggard wrote many of his early hits, Liz and Casey Anderson penned this one.
77. B) "The Long Black Veil"—Though often mistaken for a centuries-old traditional song, "The Long Black Veil" was written in 1959 by Danny Dill and Marijohn Wilkin.
78. C) "Don't Come Home A'Drinkin' (with Lovin' on Your Mind)"
79. A) "I Can't Do That Anymore"
80. C) "The King Is Gone (So Are You)"—The song's original title, "Ya Ba Da Ba Do (So Are You)," came from a trademarked Flintstones phrase.
81. D) "Murder on Music Row"—"Murder on Music Row" was nominated in both 2000 and 2001, but it won only in 2001.
82. D) "Jole Blon"—Jennings recorded the song for Brunswick in 1958.
83. C) "Waterloo"
84. C) "Here You Come Again"—In 1973, "Here You Come Again" topped *Billboard's* country chart and peaked at #3 on the pop side.
85. B) "Little Bitty"
86. A) "Abilene"—"Abilene" was Hamilton's last Top Forty pop hit, climbing to #15 in 1963.
87. B) "I Love You a Thousand Ways"
88. D) "Walkin' after Midnight"
89. D) "The Fugitive"—The song was later titled "(I'm a Lonesome) Fugitive."
90. C) "White Lightning"—The song was written by J.P. Richardson, the Big Bopper.

91. D) "I Walk the Line"—The song spent six weeks at #1 in 1956.

92. D) "You Don't Know Me"—Cindy Walker wrote the song from an idea Eddy Arnold provided her.

93. D) "You'll Never Leave Harlan Alive"

94. B) "The Great Speckled Bird"

95. B) "Where Were You (When the World Stopped Turning)"

96. B) "Southern Nights"

97. C) "Travelin' Soldier"

98. B) "How Do I Live"—Yearwood's was the bigger hit on the country chart, but Rimes's was the bigger hit on the pop side.

99. B) "The Most Beautiful Girl"

100. C) "I Love a Rainy Night"

101. A) "Dueling Banjos"

102. A) "If You've Got the Money I've Got the Time"

103. D) "Singing the Blues"

104. A) "Big Bad John"

105. A) "Lady"

106. D) "9 to 5"

107. B) "On the Other Hand"

108. D) "†9 Somethin'," Mark Wills

109. D) "Young Love"

110. A) "Baby Likes to Rock It"

111. D) "Sweet Dreams (of You)"

112. C) "Sixteen Tons"

113. C) "Country Bumpkin"

114. B) "Secret Love"

115. D) "Shameless"

116. A) "[She] He Thinks I Still Care"

117. C) "Once a Day"

118. C) "Nobody in His Right Mind Would've Left Her"

119. B) "Irma Jackson"

— NAME THAT SONG ANSWERS —

120. B) "Amos Moses"—"That's all he got left, 'cause the alligator bit it."
121. D) All of the above
122. B) "My Elusive Dreams"
123. C) "Mammas Don't Let Your Babies Grow Up to Be Cowboys"
124. C) "Pledging My Love"
125. A) "Third-Rate Romance"
126. A) "Only You (and You Alone)"
127. B) "Down Yonder"
128. C) "(Hey Won't You Play) Another Somebody Done Somebody Wrong Song"
129. D) "Sing Me Back Home"
130. C) "Rhinestone Cowboy"
131. D) "You Look So Good in Love"—Chater also co-wrote Lee Greenwood's "I.O.U.," Alabama's "If I Had You," and Reba McEntire's "You're the First Time I've Thought about Leaving."
132. B) "Lookin' for Love"
133. D) "The Bird"
134. C) "Route 66"—Wynonna changed the spelling of the Arizona town mentioned in the song's lyric: "Flagstaff, Arizona, don't forget Winona… ."
135. B) "I Don't Want to Spoil the Party"
136. D) "A Boy Named Sue"
137. B) "Patricia"
138. A) "She's Got You"
139. C) "The Whiskey Ain't Workin'"
140. B) "Forever and Ever, Amen"
141. A) "Blue Kentucky Girl"
142. C) "Just Good Ol' Boys"
143. B) "Talk to Me"—Little Willie John's single was titled "Talk to Me, Talk to Me."
144. D) "Blanket on the Ground," Billie Jo Spears
145. D) "She Called Me Baby"
146. B) "Seven Spanish Angels"
147. A) "No Love Have I"

148. B) "Old Flames (Can't Hold a Candle to You)"
149. C) "Soldier's Last Letter"
150. B) "Take Me"
151. C) "Husbands and Wives"
152. D) "Together Again"
153. C) "I Wanna Live"
154. D) "Shut Up and Kiss Me"
155. D) "Thank God I'm a Country Boy"—"I'm Sorry" also topped both charts, but "Thank God I'm a Country Boy" did it first.
156. D) "It Only Hurts When I Cry"
157. C) "Sweet Dreams (of You)"
158. A) "Bouquet of Roses," Eddy Arnold—"Bouquet of Roses" spent 53 weeks in the Top Ten during 1948 and 1949, 19 of them at #1.
159. A) "Back in the Saddle Again"
160. B) "Starting Over Again"
161. D) "Marie Laveau"
162. C) "Lucille"
163. B) "Candy Kisses"
164. B) "A Dear John Letter"—Ferlin Husky was also credited on the 1953 single.
165. C) "Skip a Rope"
166. B) "The Long Black Veil"
167. B) "Don't Worry"
168. D) "(I'd Be) a Legend in My Time"
169. A) "Abilene"
170. C) "Take Me to Your World"
171. A) "Daddy Sang Bass"
172. B) "A World of Our Own"
173. B) "She's Crazy for Leavin'"
174. A) "I Don't Want to Spoil the Party"—Though the Beatles' original made it only to #39 on the pop charts in 1965, Rosanne Cash's cover climbed all the way to the top of the country charts in 1989.

175. A) "Always Wanting You"

176. A) "I Love You Because"—Eight versions of "I Love You Because" have made *Billboard's* country charts, beginning with writer Leon Payne's, which entered on November 5, 1949.

177. A) "I Love You Because"

178. B) "One's on the Way"

179. B) "Don't Let the Stars Get in Your Eyes"

180. B) "[Today] I Started Loving You Again"—Six different artists have had country charting versions of the song, known as both "I Started Loving You Again" and "Today I Started Loving You Again"—but not Haggard.

181. A) "Born to Be with You"

182. A) "That Lovin' You Feelin' Again"—The 1980 recording was a duet with Emmylou Harris that appeared on the soundtrack for the film *Roadie*. Remakes of "In Dreams," "Oh, Pretty Woman," and "Crying" (with k.d. lang) made the charts' lower rungs, but none of Orbison's classic 1960s records were country hits.

183. A) "Almost Persuaded," David Houston

184. C) "Mountain of Love," David Houston

185. C) "Oh Lonesome Me"

186. D) "Statue of a Fool"—The song had originally been titled "Name It After Me," and Greene had held on to it for seven years.

187. C) "That's Why I Love You Like I Do"—James originally recorded the song as "You're the Reason I'm in Love" (it climbed to #6 on the country charts in 1957), but retitled it for the later recording.

188. A) "All for the Love of Sunshine"—The song was used in the 1970 Clint Eastwood film *Kelly's Heroes*.

189. B) "If You Leave Me Tonight I'll Cry," Jerry Wallace—The recording, intended to sound like Nat King Cole, was used in an episode called "The Tune in Dan's Jukebox." It was played in a jukebox that would always stick at the words "'til death."

190. D) "The Pool Shark"—"The Pool Shark" was Dudley's only #1 hit, coming in 1970.

191. A) "A Week in a County Jail"—Jackson had requested a song for an album of prison songs he was planning.

192. A) "Hello, Darlin'"—In Russian, the song is known as "Privet Radot."

193. A) "A Shoulder to Cry On"

194. B) "Had a Dream (for the Heart)"
195. A) "I Forgot More Than You'll Ever Know"—The surviving member went on to fame as Skeeter Davis.
196. A) "I Wonder If They Ever Think of Me"
197. B) "Good Hearted Woman"—Tina Turner later covered the song on one of her albums.
198. D) "The White Knight," Cledus Maggard & the Citizen's Band—Maggard was a pseudonym for Jay Huguely, who is also credited as writer.
199. A) "Linda on My Mind"
200. B) "Kentucky Gambler"
201. B) "For the Good Times"
202. D) "Would You Lay with Me (in a Field of Stone)"
203. A) "Achy Breaky Heart"
204. C) "That's the Way Love Goes"
205. C) "I'm a Ramblin' Man"
206. A) "Crazy Arms"
207. B) "Cattle Call"
208. B) "Another You"
209. B) "I Wanna Talk about Me"
210. B) "Hello Darlin'"
211. A) "My Next Thirty Years"
212. B) "Dumas Walker"
213. C) "John Deere Green"—"John Deere Green" was a Top Five hit for Joe Diffie in 1994.
214. C) "Walking the Floor over You"—Ernest Tubb released his signature hit, "Walking the Floor over You," in 1941.
215. B) "Joshua"
216. C) "Everybody Needs Love on Saturday Night"—The 1985 single on Mercury Records peaked at #24.
217. D) "Maybe I Mean Yes"—The song's lyrics included the lines, "When I say no, I mean maybe/Or maybe I mean yes."
218. D) "Fancy"

219. D) "What Kind of Love"—"What Kind of Love," which Crowell and Orbison wrote with Will Jennings, reached #11 in 1992.

220. C) "Who I Am"

221. B) "Hillbilly Shoes"

222. B) "I Feel Lucky"

223. A) "But for the Grace of God"—Urban wrote the song with band members Charlotte Caffey and Jane Wiedlin.

224. C) "He Thinks He'll Keep Her"—The slogan came from a 1970s ad campaign in which a husband proudly stated, "My wife—I think I'll keep her."

225. A) "Dance with the One That Brought You"

226. C) "What a Difference You've Made in My Life"

227. B) "The Grandest Lady of Them All"

228. D) "Take This Job and Shove It"

229. C) "Take It Easy"

230. A) "Big Four Poster Bed"—Brenda Lee's big pop hits of the early 1960s never reached the country charts.

231. D) "Only One Love in My Life"

232. B) "The Gambler"

233. A) "Every Which Way but Loose"

234. A) "The Devil Went Down to Georgia," The Charlie Daniels Band—The CDB's single actually preceded *Urban Cowboy*, but did appear on the soundtrack.

235. A) "Do Right Woman—Do Right Man"—Mandrell's band was known as the Do-Rites.

236. C) "(My Friends Are Gonna Be) Strangers"—Haggard's band is called the Strangers.

237. B) "You're My Jamaica," Charley Pride

238. B) "Honky Tonk Blues," Charley Pride—Pride's version of the song spent one week at the top of the *Billboard* country singles chart in April 1980.

239. C) "Lesson in Leavin'"—West's version came out in 1980, Messina's in 1999.

240. A) "Bar Room Buddies"—The song appeared in the Eastwood film *Bronco Billy*.

241. B) "Could I Have This Dance"—Initially, Murray recorded a second, lower voice part to be used as a guide track for a male singer; when negotiations with Rogers fell through, producer Jim Ed Norman used her harmony part on the finished version.

242. C) "Golden Ring"
243. A) "Flowers on the Wall"
244. D) "What Are We Doin' in Love?"
245. B) "Flowers on the Wall"
246. D) "Who's Cheatin' Who"—McClain's 1981 hit topped the charts; Jackson's 1997 version peaked at #2.
247. C) "I Love a Rainy Night"—The commercial debuted during halftime of the 1981 Rose Bowl.
248. B) "Lucille"—So as not to be confused with the recent Kenny Rogers hit of the same name, Jennings's version of the song was listed as "Lucille (You Won't Do Your Daddy's Will)."
249. A) "Chevy Van"—In 1988, Johns also charted with a remake of "Chevy Van" that reached only #80 on the country chart.
250. B) "Country Boy"—Dickens's band is called the Country Boys.
251. B) "She's Always Right"—McDonald wrote the song with Phil Barnhart and Ed Hill.
252. C) "Count Me In"
253. A) "Country Boy"
254. A) "Black Sheep"
255. C) "Elizabeth"—Elizabeth Taylor stars along with Rock Hudson and James Dean in the 1956 film.
256. D) "Still"
257. A) "I'm Movin' On"
258. B) "Meet Me in Montana"
259. B) "What If I Said," with Anita Cochran
260. B) "Coat of Many Colors"
261. B) "Somewhere between Ragged and Right"
262. B) "Face to Face"
263. D) "I Don't Want to Miss a Thing"
264. C) "God Ain't Gonna Getcha for That"
265. C) "Paradise Tonight"—"Paradise Tonight" spent one week atop the *Billboard* country singles chart in October 1983.
266. C) "I Ain't Never"
267. D) "Waitin' on Joe"
268. A) "Baptism"

269. A) "Big Rock Candy Mountain," Harry McClintock
270. D) "Talk Back Trembling Lips"
271. B) "How Do You Like Me Now?!"
272. D) "Six Days on the Road"—Dudley took the song the highest up the charts, reaching #2.
273. D) "Ready to Run"
274. C) "I'll Take Today"—Her name was Danette Day, and they later married. The marriage was short-lived. They split up within a few months.
275. B) "Honky-Tonk Man"
276. C) "I'm Already Taken"
277. D) "Young," Kenny Chesney
278. D) "Teddy Bear Song"
279. A) "Chasin' That Neon Rainbow"
280. A) "Man! I Feel Like a Woman!"
281. C) "The Thunder Rolls"
282. B) "When You Say Love"—Sonny & Cher had a pop hit with the song, also in 1972.
283. A) "Carlene"
284. C) "Midnight Fire"
285. D) "My Strongest Weakness"—"My Strongest Weakness" peaked at #4 in 1993.
286. B) "In the Still of the Night," The Five Satins
287. B) "Make No Mistake, She's Mine"
288. C) "Puppy Love"—Parton recorded the song at age 13 for the Louisiana-based Goldband Records. "Dumb Blonde," from 1967, was her first charting record.
289. A) "Here We Are"—Gill wrote the song with Beth Nielsen Chapman.
290. D) "That's Why I'm Here"—From this verse, which described a couple uneasy with drinking at a party, the song grew into a full lyric.
291. A) "Against the Grain"
292. D) "Touch a Hand, Make a Friend"
293. D) "Sunflower"

294. B) "I Don't Know Why You Don't Want Me"—Inspired by the loss of "Ain't No Money" to Juice Newton's "Break It to Me Gently," Cash and then-husband Rodney Crowell wrote "I Don't Know Why You Don't Want Me," which won the 1985 Best Female Country Vocal Performance Grammy.

295. C) "She Is His Only Need"

296. C) "She's in Love with the Boy"

297. B) "Could've Been Me"

298. C) "Should've Asked Her Faster"

299. C) "Sin Wagon"—The end of "Sin Wagon" features a brief quote from "I'll Fly Away," penned in 1932 by Albert E. Brumley. The song's publishers contended that the Dixie Chicks had not received permission to use the song in "Sin Wagon."

300. B) "Modern Day Bonnie and Clyde"

301. B) "Still Holding On"

302. D) "Tiny Dancer"

303. A) "Happy, Happy Birthday Baby"

304. B) "I Will Always Love You," Dolly Parton—Parton first topped the chart with the song in 1974, then again in 1982. It charted a third time for her in 1995, as a duet with Vince Gill that peaked at #15.

305. C) "Tennessee Bird Walk"

306. D) "Let's Fall to Pieces Together"

307. D) "Always Have Always Will"—After more than a decade of recording, Fricke added the "i" in an effort to stop the frequent mispronunciation of her name (it's pronounced "FRICK-ee"). "Always Have Always Will" was her last #1 hit under either name.

308. C) "The Three Bells"

309. C) "The Wanderer"

310. C) "The Thunder Rolls"

311. C) "There You'll Be"

312. A) "I Can Love You Better"

313. B) "God Must Have Spent a Little More Time on You"

314. D) "We Believe in Happy Endings"

315. A) "Country Boy"

316. B) "Someday We'll Be Together"

317. B) "Home Ain't Where the Heart Is (Anymore)"

318. B) "London Homesick Blues," Gary P. Nunn

319. C) "I Walk the Line"

320. A) "The All-American Boy"—Bare recorded the song for Parsons to learn at the end of a session, but Cincinnati-based Fraternity Records decided to release the demo. The song climbed to #2 on the pop chart in 1959.

321. B) "Goodbye Earl"

322. A) "In Another's Eyes"

323. C) "You're the Best Break This Old Heart Ever Had"—Though Bruce co-wrote "Mammas Don't Let Your Babies Grow Up to Be Cowboys," it was a #1 hit for Waylon Jennings & Willie Nelson. Bruce's original peaked at #15.

324. C) "The Change"

325. D) "José Cuervo"—As a duo with David Frizzell, West also topped the charts with "You're the Reason God Made Oklahoma" in 1981.

326. B) "I'll Never Get out of This World Alive"

327. A) "Fourteen Carat Mind"

328. B) "We Shall Be Free"—"We Shall Be Free" won the Academy of Country Music's Video of the Year award in 1994.

329. B) "It's All in Your Head"

330. B) "C-O-U-N-T-R-Y"

331. A) "Don't Let Our Love Start Slippin' Away"

332. D) "I'm Gonna Break Every Heart I Can"

333. A) "Little Bitty"

334. B) "Is There Life Out There"—Though this video won the Academy of Country Music's Video of the Year award for 1991, the lengthy sections of dialogue prompted CMT to warn country artists against making such videos in the future. The song later became the inspiration for a made-for-TV movie starring McEntire.

335. A) "I Guess You Had to Be There"

336. B) "Come Next Monday"

337. C) "Romeo"

338. C) "That's Just about Right"

339. C) "My Love"

340. A) "Honky-Tonk Superman"

341. D) "It's Only Make Believe"—Twitty's first #1 hit came on the pop charts in 1958, but it never made the country Top Forty. Glen Campbell and Ronnie McDowell both had country hits later with the song.

342. A) "Breathe"

343. C) "Holes in the Floor of Heaven"

344. A) "Forever and Ever, Amen"

345. B) "Fool Hearted Memory"

346. B) "Big River," Johnny Cash—Cash's recording of "Big River" reached #4 in 1958 and #41 12 years later when reissued by Sun Records.

347. D) "Sleeping Single in a Double Bed"

348. C) "Me and Bobby McGee"—Written by Kris Kristofferson, "Me and Bobby McGee" was a pop hit for Janis Joplin and a country hit for Roger Miller.

349. C) "Indian Outlaw"

350. B) "Honky Tonk Heart"

351. D) "Trashy Women"

352. A) "Just to See You Smile"

353. A) "Baby's Got Her Blue Jeans On"

354. B) "Austin"

355. B) "Life Turned Her That Way"

356. C) "I'd Love You All Over Again"

357. C) "Love Can Build a Bridge"

358. A) "Blame It on Your Heart"

359. A) "(This Ain't) No Thinkin' Thing"

360. A) "Don't Get Me Started"

361. B) "Jukebox in My Mind"

362. A) "Her Man"

363. A) "Still"

364. B) "The Dirt Road"

365. C) "My Name Is Bocephus"—Other people appearing in the video, which won the Country Music Association's Video of the Year award in 1987, are comedians Gallagher and Bobcat Goldthwait, and actor Dan Haggerty.
366. B) "Rose Garden"
367. B) "Southern Nights"
368. B) "Straight Tequila Night"
369. B) "Rose-Colored Glasses"
370. D) "Sorry You Asked"
371. D) "Saginaw, Michigan"—"Saginaw, Michigan" was Lefty Frizzell's last #1 hit, in 1964.
372. A) "Here in the Real World"
373. B) "If the World Had a Front Porch"
374. D) "The Letter That Johnny Walker Read"
375. C) "My Maria"
376. C) "Thinkin' Problem"
377. C) "I'm Not Strong Enough to Say No"—Robert John "Mutt" Lange wrote the song, which BlackHawk took to #2 in 1995.
378. B) "(I Wish I Had a) Heart of Stone"
379. D) "You Gave Me a Mountain"
380. B) "Hank Williams, You Wrote My Life"
381. A) "Do You Love As Good As You Look"
382. A) "A Better Man"
383. A) "Drive South"
384. D) "Leap of Faith"
385. A) "Kentucky Waltz"
386. D) "Queen of the Silver Dollar"
387. C) "'Round the Clock Lovin'"
388. D) "Passionate Kisses"
389. D) "I Still Believe in You"—"I Still Believe in You" was Gill's twenty-first Top Forty country single.
390. A) "Don't Let Me Cross Over"
391. C) "Not on Your Love"

392. A) "Baby, Don't Get Hooked on Me"—"Baby Don't Get Hooked on Me" was actually a bigger pop hit than it was a country hit, reaching the top of the pop charts but peaking at #26 on the country side.
393. B) "Every Little Thing"
394. C) "Thinkin' of a Rendezvous"
395. A) "Hank and Lefty Raised My Country Soul"
396. B) "Everybody's Free (to Get Sunburned)"—"Everybody's Free (to Get Sunburned)" parodied a pop record by movie director Baz Luhrmann called "Everybody's Free (to Wear Sunscreen)."
397. D) "We Danced Anyway"
398. A) "Ordinary Life"
399. B) "I'll Think of Something"
400. B) "Yesterday, When I Was Young"
401. C) "'Til I Gain Control Again"
402. A) "He's a Heartache (Looking for a Place to Happen)"
403. B) "Blue Blue Day"
404. B) "No News"
405. B) "Cadillac Style"
406. C) "Once in a Blue Moon"
407. A) "Alabam"—"Alabam" spent 12 weeks at #1 in 1960.
408. B) "Ruby, Baby"
409. A) "Bring It on Home to Me"
410. B) "Oklahoma Hills"
411. A) "Sing a Sad Song"
412. A) "Could've Been Me"
413. D) "Somewhere in My Broken Heart"
414. B) "I'll Get Over You"—Gayle later recorded several more of Leigh's songs, including "Your Old Cold Shoulder" and "Don't It Make My Brown Eyes Blue."
415. C) "I Don't Need Your Rockin' Chair"
416. C) "One More Day"
417. D) "Whiskey, If You Were a Woman"
418. A) "I Can Love You Better"

419. A) "Born to Run"—Though it has the same title as a famous Bruce Springsteen song, Harris's 1982 song tune was written by future husband Paul Kennerley.
420. D) "Lonesome 7-7203"
421. A) "Home"
422. C) "Daddy's Hands"
423. C) "Guitar Town"
424. B) "Little Good-Byes"
425. C) "God Bless the U.S.A."
426. B) "Give Me One More Chance"
427. C) "I'm a One-Woman Man"
428. D) "Mama's Never Seen Those Eyes"
429. C) "Crazy over You"
430. B) "Just Call Me Lonesome"
431. D) "You're the Reason God Made Oklahoma"
432. D) "Night Time Magic"
433. C) "Life to Go"
434. B) "I Ain't Living Long like This"
435. C) "Old Enough to Know Better"
436. D) "Pocket Full of Gold"
437. B) "Chiseled in Stone"
438. B) "There Goes My Everything"
439. A) "Born to Fly"
440. D) "Wild One"
441. C) "Don't Tell My Heart"
442. B) "Don't Cheat in Our Hometown"
443. B) "Cadillac Ranch"
444. D) "The Moon Is Still over Her Shoulder"
445. D) "What Mattered Most"
446. A) "I Believe in You"—"I Believe in You" was the title of separate hits for Mel Tillis and Don Williams.
447. C) "It's Just a Matter of Time"

448. A) "Whole Lot of Shakin' Going On"
449. B) "Lonely Women Make Good Lovers"
450. A) "Success"
451. B) "Eighteen Wheels and a Dozen Roses"
452. D) "You Shouldn't Kiss Me like This"
453. C) "Small Town Saturday Night"
454. D) "When You Say Nothing at All"
455. C) "Texas Tornado"
456. A) "Make the World Go Away"
457. B) "Cornell Crawford"—Though it wasn't a single until 1991, "Cornell Crawford" was actually the first song Oslin ever wrote. It was inspired by these words, scrawled on a ladies' room wall in Due West, South Carolina: "I ain't gonna love nobody but Cornell Crawford."
458. B) "Please Remember Me"
459. A) "If My Heart Had Windows"
460. D) "I'm No Stranger to the Rain"—"I'm No Stranger to the Rain," which won the Country Music Association's Single of the Year award in 1989, hit #1 on April 8, 1989, and was on the way down the charts when Whitley died. "I Wonder Do You Think of Me" entered the charts on June 24 and also went to #1.
461. C) "Southern Nights"—"Southern Nights" was written by New Orleans music man Allen Toussaint.
462. A) "Carolina in the Pines"
463. B) "Cowboy Man"
464. D) "Wild Angels"
465. B) "Heads Carolina, Tails California"
466. D) "She Thinks His Name Was John"
467. B) "Georgia on My Mind"
468. B) "Poisoned at the Well," Bob Woodruff
469. D) "Wild at Heart"
470. C) "(There's a) Fire in the Night"
471. D) "Somewhere Between"
472. A) "Once in a Very Blue Moon"

473. D) "Step by Step," Eddie Rabbitt
474. A) "Delia's Gone"
475. A) "Who's Gonna Fill Their Shoes"—"Who's Gonna Fill Their Shoes" won the Country Music Association's Video of the Year award in 1986.
476. A) "Mama Knows"—"Mama Knows" was the band's previous single.
477. A) "Gone"
478. B) "She's Got It All"
479. D) "Holdin' Heaven"
480. D) "Fool #1"—A Decca Records executive initially wanted only the song but was told he couldn't have it unless he signed Lynn. Lynn eventually released a version of "Fool #1," but it was never a single for her.
481. C) "The Thunder Rolls"
482. B) Robert Mitchum, "Little Old Wine Drinker Me"
483. A) "The Wild Side of Life"
484. C) "Crazy Little Thing Called Love"
485. C) "Shame on You"—"Shame on You" topped the charts in November 1945 (it had been a #1 hit earlier that year for Spade Cooley). The B-side of the Welk/Foley collaboration was a #3 hit, "At Mail Call Today."
486. C) "Mercury Blues"
487. B) "Tell Me Something Bad About Tulsa"—Haggard's son Noel has also recorded the song.
488. B) "He Walked on Water"—Allen Shamblin wrote "He Walked on Water," a 1990 hit for Randy Travis
489. D) "Running out of Reasons to Run"
490. A) "Charlie's Shoes"
491. C) "Evil on Your Mind"
492. A) "All-American Country Boy"
493. A) "Don't Be Cruel"
494. D) "Will the Wolf Survive?"
495. A) "I Am a Man of Constant Sorrow," The Soggy Bottom Boys—"I Am a Man of Constant Sorrow" peaked at #35 in *Billboard* Hot Country Singles & Tracks chart on April 27, 2002—more than five months after it won.

COUNTRY MUSIC
HALL OF FAME
AND MUSEUM

Accredited by the American Association of Museums, the Country Music Hall of Fame and Museum is operated by the Country Music Foundation, a not-for-profit, 501(c)3 educational organization chartered by the State of Tennessee in 1964 with a mandate to collect, preserve, and make available to the public, artifacts and information relating to the history of country music. Opened in 1967 on Music Row, the Country Music Hall of Fame and Museum relocated in May 2001 to a $37 million, state-of-the-art facility on a 3.2-acre site in the heart of Nashville's downtown entertainment district.

One of the nation's most visited museums, the 130,000-square-foot Country Music Hall of Fame and Museum illustrates the compelling history of country music using interactive media and the crown jewels of its million-item collection—costumes, films, cars, a vast collection of musical instruments, photos, documents, and sound recordings. Plaques for those elected to the Country Music Hall of Fame, the highest honor in country music, are housed in the majestic Rotunda, the heart of the new Museum. Go to the Hall of Fame's Web site, www.countrymusichalloffame.com, for a list of Hall of Fame members and biographical information on each one.

The Country Music Foundation reissues historic recordings on its own record label, publishes books, and actively investigates issues related to contemporary and historical country music performance. As a preeminent center for education, the Museum develops educational resources and programs for students, teachers, families, and adults. Tours, panel discussions, demonstrations, performances, film screenings, and other activities explore ideas and themes related to country music. The Hall of Fame Web site offers visitors an opportunity to receive, via e-mail, timely notices about events and exhibit openings at the Museum, and information useful for making travel plans.

The 6,500-square-foot Museum Store has the largest country music and book collection in Nashville and offers a wide variety of country music-related merchandise including Country Music Hall of Fame official logo apparel and souvenirs. Shoppers can visit the Museum Store without paying admission. The Museum also has an online store at www.countrymusichalloffame.com.

The Foundation is staffed by museum and library professionals and is governed by a Board of Officers and Trustees composed of executives and entertainers in the country field, business people, and community leaders.

The research and collections programs of the Country Music Foundation provide materials and consultation to the many students, journalists, and media specialists interested in country music. The heart of the Foundation's holdings is a collection of 200,000 recordings. Thousands of newspaper clippings, films, videotapes, books, and periodicals round out the collection. Dozens of network television productions and films such as *Coal Miner's Daughter* and *Tender Mercies* have made use of the research facilities at the Foundation.

A View Inside

During more than 35 years of service to researchers, country fans, the community of Nashville, and the music industry, the Country Music Foundation has expanded its ability to carry out its educational mandate. The library is unsurpassed in its coverage of country music past and present. The Foundation operates Hatch Show Print, a historic poster print shop with longtime ties to country music, and co-manages and operates historic Studio B in partnership with Belmont University. Through these activities, publications such as the *Journal of Country Music*, and teaching programs in Nashville schools, the Country Music Foundation reaches every level of interest in country music.